Caution Practical Joker Ahead

A Lifetime of Gags, Stunts, Practical Jokes, Tricks, Pranks, Stories and Other Assorted Nonsense

by Bruce Walstad

edited by Lindsay Smith

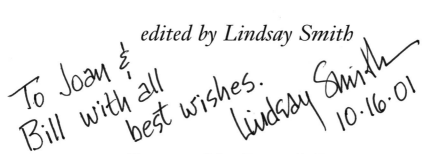

To Joan & Bill with all best wishes. Lindsay Smith 10.16.01

*Foreword by Penn Jillette –
the larger, louder half of Penn and Teller*

For information, contact Street-Smart Communications, LLC,
7275 South Depew Street, Littleton, CO 80128.

First printing, March 2001

ISBN 0-9621685-3-X

Page layout and design by Chris Stocksmith.
Illustrations by Tony Dunn, Bonita Springs, Florida.

Printed and bound in the United States of America

A disclaimer: If you plan to attempt any of these gags, tricks or practical
jokes in public, the author and publisher hereby release themselves
of any liability that may arise from individuals attempting to
recreate any of the stunts explained in this book.

Street-Smart Communications, LLC, Littleton, CO

ACKNOWLEDGEMENTS

I would like to acknowledge, with thanks, the following individuals who have inspired me through their own lifestyles that encourage this sort of nonsense...abetted me in some of my more complicated endeavors...or served as unwitting victims in some of these pranks. You know what category you fall into. Gratefully, some of you fall into more than one category...or fall into one category more than once.

Bob Andris, John Bordenet, Bob Brown, Norm Carli, Andy Dallas, Mike Deppe, Abb Dickson, John Ford, Rocky Fortino, Bill Gall, Bill Hendrickson, Glenn Hester, Ralph Iovinelli, Ricky Jay, Penn Jillette and Teller, Mac King, Mike Konwinski, Bob Little, Stan Lobenstern, Dennis Marlock, Jay Marshall, John Millner, Hank Moorehouse, Graham Mott, Tom Mullica, Bill Polka, Earl Reum, Tom Rinaldo, Todd Robbins, Colin Simpson, Lindsay Smith and Bob Steiner.

...and some departed friends, still missed: "Senator" Clarke Crandall, Karrell Fox, Jim Hoagland, Dennis Jachim, Sid Lorraine, Duke Stern.

FOREWORD BY PENN JILLETTE

The guy who wrote this goofball book is a friend of mine. He also used to be a police officer. Who needs a funny cop? Is law enforcement the place for comedy?

My Dad was in law enforcement. He was a jail guard until I was 7 years old, and remained deputy sheriff until I was in high school. My Dad was a funny guy. He was always in a good mood and he always had a joke. Working at a jail, even a little county jail in the sticks of Massachusetts, must have been pretty depressing, but my Dad and his coworkers always seemed to be laughing. I think it's an important part of the job.

One of my earliest heroes was a guy named, well, he had a great name, but who knows who has a litigious family, so I'll skip his name. You don't know him anyway. Anyway, this hero of my youth worked with my Dad at the jail. One day a new guard was hired. The new guy was that '70s cop movie cliché – the "by-the-book-rookie." We all know the type.

My hero said to my Dad, "Hey, Sam, I'm going to sneak up behind the new guy and take his gun away."

The official record shows that my Dad did not encourage this particular practical joke, but, well, no Jillette would have ever tried to stop it.

"Watch this?" said Billy (okay, I'll give you hero's first name, you dragged it out of me).

As my Dad watched, Billy moved silently across the floor of the jail office. He got behind the irritating rookie, and as my Dad watched with joy, Billy reached for the Rookie's gun. The Rookie, right by the book, spun around, and shot Billy in the stomach.

Now, up to here this story has nothing to do with the breed of cat that Bruce is. I can't imagine Bruce would ever do something this irresponsible like Billy. Bruce is very careful to explain in this book that he doesn't do the phone gags on 911. Bruce makes it clear how you should make sure that everyone has fun and no one ever gets even emotionally hurt (yeah, Bruce, most of the readers don't know you, they'll buy it).

The getting shot part is also not the part of the story that makes Billy such an inspiration to me (although it sure don't hurt). It's the next part of the story is where it gets good. What's coming up humbles us all. We can all learn from what's coming up.

Billy was gut shot, and my Dad and the Rookie had to rush him to the hospital. The doctors said it was really bad, and everyone was worried. Billy would be unconscious for a while and an in-patient for quite a while after that. My Dad and the Rookie were in the room when Billy came to for the first time after he was shot. Billy had been out for a while. Billy knew he'd been shot. The pain was incredible. He knew he was in the hospital. But, get this. This is the hero part. I love this – he came to laughing. Billy woke up laughing. Really laughing. He was laughing so hard it hurt. He was looking at the Rookie and laughing.

"Man, you are good, kid. Right by the book, you shot me. Yup, well done. Sam, wasn't that great how I snuck up behind him? But, he shot me. He's fast. He's good. Well, done, Kid. Wasn't that funny? Wasn't that great? Am I going to be okay?"

Billy told the story to everyone. And every time he'd tell it, he'd laugh. He was shot in the stomach, but he laughed. It hurt like a bastard, but he laughed.

The boss at the jail, the sheriff, said to Billy, "You know, Billy, I might have been stupid enough to think of a stunt like that, but I'd never be stupid enough to really do it. And if I were stupid enough to really do it, I'd never tell anyone about it."

And Billy laughed. And the Rookie laughed. And my Dad laughed every time he told Billy's story.

My buddy, Bruce, has collected practical jokes from all over. Some he made up, some were made up by his buddies, some are from books, some use props you buy at a joke shop. Bruce puts them in context. He tells you how to really use them in the real world. He tells you how to pick a person who will understand the joke and really enjoy it. He tells you to be really careful.

Bruce was a police officer. He's to be trusted. He's responsible. These are all jokes that are created with love, in the purest of human kindness. Bruce is a good man, with good ideas.

And when you come to, try to be laughing.

Penn Jillette

Table of Contents

"The gods too are fond of a joke."

Aristotle (384 – 322 B.C.)

INTRODUCTION

Ever since I was a young boy, I have enjoyed gags and practical jokes. Over the years I have become an able practitioner of such nonsense, much to the chagrin of my family, friends, co-workers and occasional stranger.

At a recent family get-together my brother, Dennis, suggested to me that I should write a book about all the practical jokes I have pulled over the years, as he had always found my stories about my gags and jokes entertaining. The more I thought about it, the more I thought why not? So I decided to share some of my tales of mischief.

It has always been my philosophy to never damage anything or hurt anyone physically with a practical joke or gag. Although I will admit that I may have injured the pride or wounded the egos of a few people now and again. But overall, I have found most recipients of my foolishness take it quite well. There are some people we all know who just can't take a good joke. I generally leave these people alone, most of the time.

This book contains my personal collection of jokes, gags, practical jokes, stunts and sight gags. Some of these ideas are of my own creation.

Many others are tried and true bits of business or store-bought items that I have added my ideas to. Friends showed others to me. I claim no originality for most of this material, and I've tried to give credit to the creator or the person who showed me the bit. I also must add that I have pulled many other gags and jokes that are just too complicated, off color or politically incorrect to put in print.

Over the years I've developed a number of "favorite" practical jokes that have served me well, and most of them are noted as such in the pages to follow. But my all-time favorite -- the one that undoubtedly will hook the most victims -- is the one that appears on pages 46-47 in this book. Don't overlook this one.

Some of these gags can be done almost spur-of-the-moment, with no advance set-up. Others will require some preparation ahead of time. However, it's been my experience that the payoff on the gag almost always exceeds the time and energy invested in the preparation. For me, it's always been worth whatever effort was necessary.

One of the keys to the success of running a gag or a practical joke is finding the right "victim." I have found that some people, for whatever reason, just don't see it coming. These are my favorite people. Others, though, see it coming a mile off and the joke falls flat. For example, my good friend and former lieutenant, Rocky Fortino, was very skeptical of everything. I don't think I ever got him on anything during the years we worked together. However, I did use him unwillingly in several practical jokes at the station that I will tell you about later. On the other hand, there were several other officers I worked with who fell for almost everything I tried on them. Whenever I had a new gag in mind, I was usually eager to get to work.

Another important aspect of making these jokes and gags work is the ability to keep a straight face. Many of my victims will attest to the fact that I can do this pretty well. I've found that the best way to present many of these gags is by looking as surprised as the victim by the unusual goings-on. I'm usually right there with him, with a puzzled look on my face, thinking, "Now how could something like that happen?"

The all-important disclaimer:

OK, here comes the disclaimer. I'm not suggesting that you actually do any of the stuff described in this book. I put this collection of mischief together just to share some of my stories of things that just seem to happen when I'm nearby (or sometimes not). I will take no responsibility for any trouble you might get in through any attempt to follow in my errant footsteps.

To my fellow police officers: If you get called into the chief's office, get a letter of reprimand put in your files or get suspended for pulling any of this nonsense around your department, don't blame me or call me; you are on your own.

SIGHTS & SOUNDS

"You can pretend to be serious; you can't pretend to be witty."

--Sacha Guitry (1885-1957)

Sight gags are among my favorite bits of business. I have found that doing this strange visual stuff in front of people usually stimulates interesting and humorous reactions. My favorite sight gags are all here, followed by jokes and gags that incorporate both sound and visuals.

Cup on the Car Roof

Imagine driving around town with a plastic drinking cup from a fast-food restaurant sitting on the top of your car, just above the driver's side door. Even at 30 miles an hour, it doesn't fall off. Meanwhile, people in cars behind you, next to you (and sometimes oncoming) will begin honking, waving,

yelling or pointing at the cup on your roof. You'll get amazing reactions from people trying to get your attention because they all think you're an idiot who put his cup on the roof to dig out his car keys, then got in the car and forgot about the cup.

When they honk, I smile and wave at them. When they wave their arms to get my attention, I sometimes ignore them for a while, then finally smile and wave back. When they point, I act puzzled. I raise my hands, palm up, as if to say, "Huh?"

I'm not quite sure where I first learned this. It seems to me I have seen variations of this in joke books and novelty catalogs.

Here is my version: You need a powerful magnet and a plastic cup. The magnet I use is about one half inch thick and about three inches in diameter, and it just fits the bottom of my cup. I use a strong rare-earth magnet that you can pick up at your local science supply company for a couple of dollars.

The cup I use is from TCBY, which I chose simply because of its bright, attention-grabbing colors. Just place the magnet in the bottom of the empty cup, place the cup on the roof of your car and drive away. You can drive at speeds up to 30 or 40 MPH and the cup will not move. (Those of you driving convertibles can skip the rest of this and proceed directly to the next gag.)

My friend and former partner, Norm, ran this gag a few times. I recall one time where a guy in a dump truck was chasing after us beeping his horn. When we stopped for a traffic light, he jumped out of the truck, ran up to our car and told Norm he had left a cup on the roof. When he went to pick it up and hand it to Norm he figured out the gag. He laughed and walked away shaking his head.

On another occasion, I remember I had put the cup on the roof of a friend's car. There were several people in the car and I had placed the cup over the left rear door.

The guy sitting in the back had no idea the cup was there. As they drove off, passing motorists were waving and pointing at the cup. The guy in the back had no idea what was going on, so he waved back.

This is enormously funny stuff for a minimal investment. As the commercial says, don't leave home without it.

You Have an Insect Problem

Sometimes, in rooms where I've been, as a door is opened or closed, a cockroach runs across the floor, seemingly following the door's path. Sometimes women scream. Go figure.

This is a bit I learned at Dallas and Company, a magic store in Champaign, Illinois. Wes, the store manager, showed me this one.

You need to get a rubber or plastic cockroach (the bigger the better). The one I have is about two inches in length. You tie one end of a 12" piece of clear sewing thread to the head of the cockroach and fasten a small ball of wax to the other end.

Now stick the ball of wax on the bottom edge of the door, on the opening side, and run the thread along the bottom of the door and lay the cockroach next to the door. When the door is then opened or closed, the cockroach will appear and run after the door.

I first tried this in the lobby of a hotel in Shreveport, Louisiana, on the door to the women's washroom. I was conducting a law enforcement lecture in Shreveport and, during a break, I was telling some of the officers attending about this new gag. They urged me to try it out, so I gave in and hooked it up on the women's washroom door. Within two minutes we heard a shriek, and I knew it was a winner.

Since that time, I have run this gag on many unsuspecting people. One of my favorite victims was a custodian at a police department who, after seeing the cockroach run after the door, ran to get his can of Raid.

Wes also told me it also works equally well when the cockroach is placed in a desk drawer and the wax is attached to desk, so that when the drawer is opened it appears the cockroach is running inside the drawer.

When you find the cockroach you like, I suggest you buy at least a half dozen. You'll need them.

Rock in the Shoe

Quite often when I'm with people, it's amazing how many times I'll come up lame and start limping. Sometimes it happens when I'm on a platform lecturing, usually just after returning from lunch, but other times, it happens when I'm just walking around with a small group. It can happen anywhere. I explain to the people I'm with that it feels like I've got a rock or a pebble in my shoe. So then I stop, remove my shoe and shake out a rather large rock.

Next time you're in your local novelty or magic shop (you'll learn to love these stores), ask them if they have the foam rubber rocks. The ones I use are usually gray, a few inches long, by a couple inches wide, and an inch or so thick. They come in different shapes and sizes and are surprisingly realistic. They look like real granite. They compress down to maybe a quarter inch.

The set up is quite easy: Just put the rock in your shoe and then put your shoe on. (I wear slip-ons, which make getting the shoe on and off much easier.) I have been doing this bit for at least 20 years and have no idea where I got the idea. I have done this so often over the years, I could not even venture a guess as to how many times I have come up lame. The reaction is always entertaining, by both children and adults.

What adds to this bit is that you have to look very bewildered when the rock appears. You can then mention something about returning it to the parking lot later.

Money to Burn

You can't imagine the number of times I've gone into a restaurant, gotten the attention of the hostess, removed my wallet from my pocket and, as I opened it, had the inside of the wallet burst into flames! I am always surprised when this happens.

The Fire Wallet is a standard dealer item at most magic shops. They range in price from $25 to $50, depending on the manufacturer. I purchased my first fire wallet at least 15 years ago, and used it from time to time in my magic show with positive results.

However, it was not until I met Earl Reum of Denver a few years ago that I realized the full potential of this gag. Earl is a magician, professional speaker, student council workshop leader and one of the funniest people you'll ever meet.

I watched from the sidelines as Earl whipped out his wallet and had it burst into flames with just about every stranger he came in contact with. The reaction of the onlookers was one of shock and amazement. From that moment on, I carried my fire wallet most everywhere I went.

I have added a few bits of business I will share with you.

When I go to a restaurant with friends, I take out my wallet as I enter and tell the cashier or hostess that I am buying. (The line here is, "…because I have money to burn,") as I activate the wallet and the fire appears. The usual reaction is that their eyes get big, they jump backward or their jaw drops, and sometimes all of the above. This is followed by, "Do that again."

I do the same bit when the waiter or waitress comes to the table or when I am paying the check. Sometimes I will just ask a stranger for change for a large bill and have the wallet burst into flames.

One of the most unusual reactions I ever got was in Connecticut when I was out to dinner with a lieutenant of the Connecticut state police. As we walked into the restaurant, I produced the wallet and gave the standard line to the hostess about having money to burn and that I was buying as the wallet burst into flames. She jumped back and yelled out. She asked me to do it again, so I did. As the wallet was burning, she started reaching into the flames with her hand and asked if that was real fire. Needless to say I closed the wallet and immediately started to think of what other gags I could pull on her.

A few words of warning here. Be very careful with the fire wallet. You can easily burn yourself, your clothing or someone else. If you purchase a fire wallet, read the directions carefully. Also, don't heavily drench the wick with lighter fluid and then put the wallet in your pocket, or you will wind up with a chemical burn on your bottom side.

Don't ask me how I know.

Sparks at Your Fingertips

I have many favorite bits of business and this is one of them. The sparker – also known as a Funken Ring or a Spark Ring – is a standard item available at most magic and novelty shops. It is a small metal device that fits in the palm of your hand. You wind it up like a child's toy and when the button or trigger is pushed, it emits a shower of sparks for about one second. There are various models available, ranging in price from $10 to $75. The $75 model is powered by an electric motor. I have at least one of each.

If you stop and think about it, the possibilities of this device are endless. I use it frequently on telephones, light switches, light fixtures and police radios. One of my favorite uses is on a crowded elevator. Just get on, hit your floor button, let the shower of sparks go and jump back. The elevator empties out in a hurry and you can ride, usually by yourself, to your floor.

I have used this device in so many different ways, I actually can't recall them all, but a few amusing incidents come to mind.

On one occasion, I was in Baton Rouge, Louisiana, teaching for a group of police officers. The director of training asked me if I needed to use the PowerPoint system. I told him no, and then he reminded me not to mess with it as he had just purchased it for big bucks. He probably shouldn't have told me that.

About two hours later he came back into the classroom and I complained to him about a shock I had received from the PowerPoint projector. He told me that was impossible. The class was in on the gag, and a few of the officers helped me by saying that it had indeed given me a shock. I then reached over to the PowerPoint projector, touched it and at the same moment pushed the button of the sparker emitting a stream of sparks about eight inches from the projector. I jumped up and yelled.

The director had a look of horror on his face and I think his heart skipped a beat. Then the class started laughing. He was a good sport and, after realizing he had "been had," he approached me after class and asked where he could get one.

Another incident occurred in a restaurant I was in with a group of police officers following a seminar. I noticed a piece of conduit coming out of a junction box near some stairs in the dining area. I called the waitress over and told her I had dropped something on the floor and while trying to pick it up, brushed the junction box and had gotten a shock. She said to show her where.

As I bent down, I touched the junction box and set off the sparker. The sparks flew out and I jumped back. She then started telling me how stupid I was

11

to do it again and walked away. A few minutes later she returned with the manager, who I think was a bit skeptical of what was going on. He asked me what happened and again I reached for the junction box and let the sparks fly. The waitress again starting telling me how stupid I was to keep shocking myself.

The manager figured out it was a gag and laughed, as did the officers present. The waitress then realized she had been the victim of a prank and pushed me and twisted my arm. The officers watching thought that this was quite amusing, and were actually encouraging the waitress to do bodily harm to me. The manager returned later to ask how I did that and where he could get one.

Magic dealer, magician, friend and funny man Bob Little of Hatboro, Pennsylvania, showed me this off-color bit a few years ago, and I admit I have used it from time to time. As you'll see, you need to pick the right audience and occasion for this one. It's not for everyone.

You have the sparker in your right hand and then unzip your pants. You place your right hand (with the sparker facing outward) in front of your open zipper and say, "Here is my impression of an electrician taking a leak." You then let the sparks fly. In the right place, at the right time, for the right audience, it's hilarious.

P.S. Don't forget to zip up while everyone's laughing.

Here are my favorite gags that incorporate both sound and visuals.

I Didn't Know That Squeaked

Can you imagine being in front of any kind of display of virtually any kind of merchandise and having the items squeak when you touch them? It happens to me all the time.

A hand squeaker is a small plastic device that fits in your hand. When you squeeze it, it makes a squeaking noise. You can purchase squeakers at most magic shops for less than a dollar. I buy these in bulk quantity, as I tend to lose them or give them away. I have been using squeakers for years and rarely leave home without one in my pocket.

Anything can squeak. Neckties, cuff links, tie tacks, elevator buttons, all toys (this drives children crazy), phone buttons, computer or typewriter keys, small animals, coat sleeves, sugar packets, dinner rolls, walls and anything else you can think of.

Here are a few of my favorite squeaker stories:

My former partner and friend, Norm, and I were leaving a restaurant with another detective who was paying the check. While standing at the cash register I noticed a rubber change mat with four credit card logos printed on it. I got my squeaker in place and started pushing on the credit card logos with my index finger. When I pushed on the fourth logo, it squeaked! I was surprised.

I saw the manager and cashier looking puzzled at what had just happened. I repeated the process and again, the fourth logo squeaked. I looked puzzled too, shrugged my shoulders and we started to walk out. As we were leaving, the manager picked the change mat off the counter and started squeezing the logos, commenting to the cashier, "I didn't know it did that."

No, I never told him.

On another occasion, I was in my local credit union and noticed a number of small rubber cars on the counter with some sort of imprint about a loan deal they were offering. I got out the squeaker and casually picked up the car closest to me, squeezed it and naturally it squeaked. I squeaked it a few times and then replaced it on the counter. Instantly, all the tellers picked up the cars near them and started squeezing them.

The head teller was at just the right angle (or maybe the wrong angle) to spot the squeaker in my hand. I can still see her just shaking her head as all the tellers were squeezing all the rubber cars.

My favorite squeaker incident occurred in Orlando, Florida, in Disney World's Animal Kingdom. My wife, Pat, had purchased a small box of candy from a vendor. My wife was looking at something else as the clerk rang up the sale and got her change. I saw him pick up a big rubber cockroach and place it on top of the box of candy. He then handed the box to my wife, I suspect hoping to startle her. My wife, who has been through a lot of been there, done that, thought it was amusing and handed me the cockroach. Pretty soon the cockroach began to squeak when I squeezed it.

The vendor looked puzzled and told me he had been playing with these things for months and he did not know they squeaked. I handed it back to him and started walking away. He immediately started squeezing the cockroach. We got about ten steps away when he called me back, asking me how I got it to squeak.

I had to retrieve my squeaker, which was in my pants pocket. I was trying to kill time because I could not get the squeaker out of my pocket, so I told the vendor you have to squeeze its butt, which he immediately started doing. With that remark my wife walked away just shaking her head. Eventually I got the squeaker out of my pocket and had the cockroach squeaking again. The vendor thanked me for showing him and I walked away. I got about 50 feet away this time and looked back to see the vendor busily squeezing cockroaches' butts.

No, I did not tell him.

Mouth Squeaker

As you pull up your chair at a restaurant and sit down, the chair cushion begins making a loud squeaking noise. Pick up a tissue and start to blow your nose and a high-pitched squeaky noise occurs. Squeeze a purse or suitcase and it begins making a strange, almost animal-like crying noise. All these things (and many more) are possible when you have this squeaker.

This little device is like the ones found in dog squeaky toys. You can buy them from some magic shops and they cost about fifty cents each. The ones I use are made of hard, clear plastic about a half-inch long and about a quarter-inch in diameter.

This squeaker is worked from your mouth. It will make various types of sounds depending on how hard you blow into it and which end you blow into to. You will need to practice with it to determine how to make the different sounds.

I got my first squeaker from Bob Little about 10 years ago. I have been using it since, doing various gags.

My favorite is blowing my nose as described above. This squeaker, along with my hand squeaker and watch winder, are always in my pocket when I leave the house.

Earl Reum is the true master of this device. One of Earl's favorite bits is to pick up a fork or spoon at the dinner table and pretend to play it like a flute, using the squeaker to make all sorts of musical noise. Waiters and waitresses are amazed and his dining companions are amused.

One of the funniest things I saw Earl do with this was at a hotel. As we were unloading his luggage from a car, Earl told the bellboy to be careful with a particular suitcase. As he was telling this to the bellboy, he bent down and squeezed the sides of the suitcase at which time animal crying noises apparently came from within the suitcase.

The bellboy's eyes widened and he had this shocked expression on his face. I recall the bellboy picked up all the other suitcases, leaving the one with the animal in it for Earl to carry.

Here is a new idea that my friend, Rich Viken, gave me. While writing on a chalkboard, with your back to the audience, use the squeaker to make some really terrible squeaky noises. I tried it; it works!

Here are a few tips for using the mouth squeaker:

Always cover your mouth or turn your face away from the viewers so they can't see the squeaker sticking out of your mouth.

If you keep the squeaker in your mouth for an extended period of time, it tends to fill up with saliva and become inoperable. If this happens, simply take it out and put it in your pocket. It will dry out in a short time.

Lastly, and most important, be careful not to swallow this device. I have yet to do that, but it could happen.

Watch Winder

Most people I encounter think I have a really cheap watch. It constantly runs down or stops when I'm out in public, and when I go to wind it up, it makes this horrendous ratcheting noise that sounds just awful.

Everybody needs a watch winder. The watch winder is a small metal device that can easily be concealed in the palm of your hand. It has a small gear protruding from it that you rotate with your thumb and that's what creates the noise. This is also a standard item found in most magic shops. The prices range from $1 to $15. Generally speaking, the more expensive they are, the louder the sound. Louder is better, but even the less expensive models will serve you well. I have carried a watch winder in my pocket for many years. Like the squeaker, I rarely leave home without one.

This is my opening gag in my lectures, at restaurants or with people I just met. I usually ask people for the correct time, explaining that my watch stopped. When they tell me the time, I pretend to wind my watch. Most people laugh, but from time to time some will ask, quite concerned, "Is that really your watch making that noise?" In either case I respond by saying, "It's a cheap watch, but it generally keeps good time."

You can also use the watch winder when sitting down or standing up, pretending that your back is making the noise. Earl Reum uses the watch winder when he straightens out the knot of his necktie.

This is a must-have item. I have worked this bit literally thousands of times and it always produces laughs and looks of amazement. I've found that the best watch winders are available from Bob Little or Hank Moorehouse.

Here's a tip: To work the watch winder correctly, place it in the hand that you wear your watch on, not the hand you are pretending to be winding the watch with.

Everything's a Radio

Several years ago at a magic convention in Colon, Michigan, magic dealer Al Cohen asked to borrow my pen. He looked it over, then asked, "Is this one of those pens that plays music?" He twisted the cap a little and sure enough, my pen began playing music! Then he turned it off and handed it back to me. In Al's hands, anything will play music: pens, pencils, silverware, you name it.

This is an item I had heard of for several years and finally bought after Al showed it to me. I have not worked with it a lot, but when I have the results have been great.

The name of the trick is A.M. Ink or, Everything's A Radio. Al has the sole marketing rights to this trick and the only place you can buy one is from Al's Magic Shop in Washington, D.C. The trick is worth obtaining. At the time this book went to press, the price was $85, including batteries and a tape.

Since Al is marketing this great effect by George Farmer, I'm not at liberty to explain how it works, but I can tell you that it uses a micro-cassette recorder. For even more versatility, you can program your own favorite music into it or even some static as you pretend to be searching the dials for another station.

With this device, anything you can pick up and fiddle with becomes a radio and plays music. I have found pens to be the best, and I do it much as Al first showed it to me. You borrow a pen from someone, or use your own, and proceed to twist the cap around, and the music begins playing. It's just about as simple as that. Al has another routine where he borrows two coins, rubs them together and they start playing music.

Another great gag that Al does with it is to draw a picture of a radio on the back of his business card. He then pretends to turn it "on" and it starts playing. Then he turns it off and gives it to someone as a souvenir. It's a neat way to give someone your card.

This is one of those great tricks where you're limited only by your own imagination.

Back-Cracking Bottle

Lecturing is hard work. You're on your feet most of the time and that can cause lower-back pain. When I'm on the platform and that happens to me, I wiggle around a little and as I straighten up my back, there's a horrible cracking sound. It always helps.

This is an idea I came up with several years ago, and your investment is minimal. You need a 16- or 20-ounce plastic Coca-Cola bottle. After you have consumed the Coke, wash out the bottle. Next, squeeze some of the air out of the bottle and tightly recap the bottle. By squeezing the bottle now, it makes very loud cracking noises. Try it.

To work the gag, place the bottle, neck down, in the back of your pants, so the bulk of the bottle is sticking out above your belt line. Start talking about the lower back pain you get. Reach behind you with one hand and grab the bottle, bend your body forward and as you straighten back up, squeeze the bottle repeatedly. The effect is always enhanced if you have a pained expression on your face as you're going through this. The reaction is always interesting to say the least.

I have done this bit hundreds of times. Some of the more interesting reactions have been: "Are you OK?" "Don't move, I'll get help!" "You need to see a doctor!" "Is that really your back?"

I have found that other soft drink or water bottles work OK, but for some reason Coca-Cola bottles have the best sound. Go for the real thing.

Electronic Whoopee Cushion

At one time or another, just about every kid has had a Whoopee Cushion, that flat red rubber balloon that you partially inflate and put under a chair cushion. When your victim sits down, it sounds as if they have "passed gas." I had one (actually, many) when I was a kid; maybe you did too.

Now, thanks to modern technology, this ancient joke has gotten better than ever. The electronic version is a standard item you can purchase from any novelty or magic shop. The price is about $15 to $20. It consists of a small wireless transmitter with a button on it, and a battery-powered receiver unit, which has a digital player and speaker in it.

One of the advantages of the electronic version over the old inflatable cushion is the multiple-use feature. The cushion could only be used once before you had to blow it up again. The electronic version will continue repeating just by pushing the button.

You attach the receiver unit under the chair of your proposed victim (when they are not around) and you are ready to go. You can also place it behind a pillow if it's on a couch (as long as you don't muffle the sound). By merely pushing the button on your transmitter, it activates the receiver, which emits one of four individual, very realistic, "passing gas" sounds. I use these so often, I have actually worn out a few of these over the years.

John Ford, fellow officer at the Franklin Park Police Department, has reminded me on several occasions how I had placed the electronic whoopee cushion under his seat at one of my seminars he was attending and embarrassed him in front of a room full of cops.

Probably the funniest incident with this device occurred at a law-enforcement conference I was attending in Milwaukee. During a break, I placed the receiver in the coat pocket of a friend, Glenn Hester, while he was out of the room. He had left his sports coat draped over his chair. I told the instructor what I had planned and he went along with the gag. Glenn, incidentally, was sitting next to two women who were not in on the gag and had not seen me "load" his coat.

Soon after we were back in session, the instructor stopped talking to pick something up and I hit the button. Everyone looked in Glenn's area and he started laughing. The two women next to Glenn did not laugh.

A few minutes later the instructor paused, and I pushed the button again. Glenn started laughing and this time turned around and looked at the guy sitting behind him, thinking he was the one passing gas. At this point, the two women sitting next to Glenn were giving him dirty looks and were slowly, but quite deliberately, edging their chairs away from Glenn. This continued three or four more times. Each time Glenn laughed, looked at the guy behind him and the women moved further away. Glenn has a marvelously expressive face when he's puzzled and this was definitely one of those times. I was in stitches.

At the next break and right in front of Glenn, I retrieved the receiver from his coat pocket. It was hard to tell, but I think he found this somewhat amusing. But he insisted that I show the device to the women next to him and explain that he wasn't the one making those noises.

Think of this as a new version of "musical" chairs.

2

AROUND THE TOWN

"Everybody likes a kidder, but nobody lends him money."

--Arthur Miller

These are all gags and bits of business that you can do when you're out and about, from over at the neighbor's house to out on the street.

Rare Moving Mushroom

My former next-door neighbor, Reggie, was an easy mark. Once I found that out, you can imagine what happened. I pulled a few pranks on him and he fell for them all. My favorite was what I called the "Moving Mushroom."

I used to tease Reggie about his lawn, because there were mushrooms growing all over his lawn in the summer months. Somehow I came across a bunch of three plastic mushrooms about five inches tall. I inserted a metal rod in the stem and planted the bunch next to his garage.

About a week later I moved them to a different spot next to the garage about five feet away. I kept this up for several weeks until I saw Reggie out mowing his lawn. As I watched, he stopped mowing, walked over to the mushrooms, looked at them for a minute or so, shook his head and went back to his mowing.

The next day I moved them again. Believe it or not, this actually went on most of the summer until he did a more thorough inspection and discovered that they were fakes. He came to my door (go figure) with the mushrooms in hand, laughing. He explained to me that he could not figure out how those mushroom that were growing and dying next to his garage always looked alike. He said he even brought his wife outside a couple of times to look at them. Finally, he asked if he could keep the mushrooms; he wanted to use them on a friend's lawn.

Animal in the Bushes?

While you are walking down a sidewalk, passing a home that has hedges or bushes alongside, suddenly strange, almost animal-like noises come from the bushes. You look and see nothing.

If I recall, my brother, Dennis, came up with this one a long time ago. I used it on and off for years, especially at Halloween.

All you need is a speaker, an amplifier and a microphone. Hide the speaker in the bushes next to the sidewalk and run the wires to the amplifier in the house. You are now ready to startle and maybe scare any passersby.

The house I lived in as a child had hedges along the front sidewalk. We used to set this up, turn out the lights in the house and watch out the front windows for people walking by. When the person got close we would scratch on the microphone and make quiet snorting noises. When they would stop and start to look for the source, we would snort a little louder.

Some people would just walk away, others would jump and if I remember right, a few came to the front door to complain to my mother. Halloween was always the perfect night for this as no one ever complained.

New Silverware?

This gag amuses me, even though the puzzlement happens after you have departed the scene. Let's assume that you've attended a dinner, a party or some other get-together at the home of a friend or relative. Later that evening, after you and the other guests have left, the hostess finds one or two pieces of odd silverware as she's putting things into the dishwasher. As a matter of fact, every time these people have guests over, more new pieces of unmatched silverware appear.

Actually I did this by accident once and the idea was born. The mind works in mysterious ways – at least mine does.

When I'm performing close-up magic, I do several tricks with silverware and often have a few pieces in my case of magic. One time I was doing some magic at a friend's house and accidentally left a couple spoons behind.

I got to thinking they must be wondering where these new spoons came from. I was also thinking, on my next visit I will leave a few more pieces behind.

You can buy odd and inexpensive pieces of silverware at most dollar stores. I have found you can sometimes get a complete place setting for a buck. Neighborhood garage sales also are a great source for odd pieces of silverware.

While you're at the party or dinner, just slip the extra silverware into the sink with the other dirty dishes and silverware. I suspect if you did this repeatedly to the same people, you would leave them really wondering.

And who knows? They might like your pattern better than what they're currently using.

One-Way Glass

This is an excellent gag to use when someone you know moves into a new home.

One day the new homeowners get an anonymous post card that reads as follows: "A group of your neighbors would like to advise you that the frosted, one-way glass in your bathroom has been installed backwards."

Lindsay Smith is responsible for telling me about this one. I tried this

23

out a few times and it had really interesting results. Many people will get the gag right away; others might have to think about that for a few minutes, (could that really be the case?).

One person I sent the card to fell for this in a big way. He told me he had his wife standing in front of the window one evening, while he was out in the backyard looking up at it from different angles. Then he had his wife steam up the bathroom window with the shower, thinking maybe the window needed to have moisture on it.

Eventually he figured out the window was not installed backwards, nor could it be. He came to me and asked me what I knew about it. That's when he admitted what he had done. As silly as this sounds, people do fall for this. Try it.

Honk, It's My Birthday

Sometimes, as my friends drive around in their cars, people they don't even know will honk and wave at them for no apparent reason. It's all very puzzling to them…until they figure it out. It could happen to your friends too.

All you need is a computer and some self-stick 8 1/2" x 11" sheets of paper. Use your favorite sign-making program (I use Broderbund's The Print Shop) to make up a sign reading, "Honk, It's My Birthday." The size of the layout should be about 10" long by 3" high. Make sure you select a large, easy-to-read typeface.

You will be able to get two stickers per sheet. If you want, you can also add some birthday type graphics. All you need to do now is place one of the stickers on the back of a friend's car.

I came up with this idea about four or five years ago. From time to time I have placed the stickers on cars of my friends at work. My former partner, Norm Carli, eventually found the sticker on his car after a couple days and came to work the next day complaining and blaming me.

He went on to explain that over the past couple days, several people who had been driving behind him were honking at him and a few even waved. He told me he had no idea what was going on and that it was really irritating him.

I never knew what led him to suspect me…except he was a detective.

Talking Beanie Babies?

Did you know that Beanie Babies could talk? I sure didn't, until Don Wiberg gave me this idea.

While you are at a store or flea market looking at a display of Beanie Babies, you pick one up and squeeze it and it starts talking, much to your surprise and the people standing around you.

For this funny bit, you need one of those small digital memo recorders. I picked mine up at Radio Shack for about $10. Mine is small enough so it can be easily hidden in the palm of my hand.

Then I had a friend at work put a short recording on it: "Hi, I am a talking Beanie Baby. Tickle my tummy and make me laugh."

To work this, palm the recorder and then pick up a Beanie Baby and start looking at it. Activate the recorder to play the message, and lay the Beanie Baby on top of the recorder and listen as it talks. Look surprised and then put it back.

Don tells me he did this in a department store with a stuffed animal. He said it got quite an interesting response from the women shoppers who were trying to find the talking one among all the other animals.

As of this writing I have yet to try this out, but I can't wait to get to a flea market.

Remote Control Madness

This device can produce some pretty annoying results, which is reason enough to have one.

While you're watching a TV or a video with friends, suddenly the volume goes way up, the channel changes, the volume goes way down or the tape starts rewinding. What's up with that?

You too can annoy your friends with the Casio TV/VCR Remote Control Wristwatch.

One of my son's friends showed me this watch a while back. I thought it was great and my wife bought me one for my birthday a few months later.

Although I have used it from to time, my son, Omar, is the master of this gag. Anytime we would go to a department store or an electronics store, unusual things would start to happen in the TV section. His favorite ploy was turning up the volume of several TVs.

I remember one day particularly well. I was shopping with my sons, John and Omar, at a department store and Omar had wandered off. John and I were in the front of the store waiting to leave and wondering where Omar was, and then we noticed that we could hear the TV audio coming from the rear of store. A moment later Omar walked up laughing. We made a quick exit.

Three years ago, Omar and I went to Abbott's Magic Company in Michigan for a magic convention. Less than two hours after arriving, Omar was at work with the remote control watch.

In the showroom, Abbott's had several TV sets with VCRs set up playing various magic instructional videotapes they were offering for sale. Omar alternated between turning the volume up, then down, up, down. He also stopped the tapes now and then and rewound them several times. Hank Moorehouse, the guy in charge of the convention, started noticing all the changes in the TV's volume and told the employees to stop messing with the audio levels.

They all pleaded innocent because they were. Since the TVs and VCRs were just brought over to the showroom for the convention, they were concerned that maybe they'd hooked up the wiring wrong or something.

Omar kept it up and Hank was getting just a bit upset. I recall seeing Hank trying to show a magician one segment of a particular videotape, but the tape kept alternating between rewind and fast-forward.

By this time several other magicians had caught on to what Omar was up to and when Hank would walk into the room, they would have to walk out for fear of laughing. From time to time Omar would pass the watch to me and I would assist.

This went on for several hours and came to an abrupt end when a TV repairman (called from a repair shop 40 miles away) showed up to fix whatever was wrong. Omar later confessed to Hank, and I can recall him saying to Omar, "I knew it was you!"

The following year I went to the convention alone. As soon as Hank

spotted me soon after my arrival, he approached me and asked if Omar was with me. I told him no, and Hank replied, "Good!"

These Casio watches cost about $60 or $70, and have the ability to control just about any make of TV or VCR. The only problem is finding the correct codes to operate the various makes and models. Omar has developed a method of searching and can usually get the code in less than a minute.

You could also do this gag with any universal programmable remote control. The only problem with this is the size. It would be hard to conceal.

Elusive Red Dot

About five or six years ago, I was one of the first kids on the block to have a laser pointer. It quickly became another of those "don't leave home without it" items. A couple years later, the price dropped on them and you could buy a laser pointer for $10. I had so much fun with it and so many laughs, I was sorry to see them become so popular. I have since abandoned my laser gags, but still use it to play with my cat.

The gag I pulled most often with the laser was to point it at the ground near the feet of children and move the dot around. I had a method of concealing the laser in my hand with my arms folded and no one could determine the source. The children would chase it, step on it, swat it and try to catch it. Adults would often get involved and wonder what that red dot was. A few memorable occurrences come to mind.

I was at a restaurant with my partner and noticed the bus boy standing by a counter folding napkins. I got out the laser and aimed it on the floor in front of his feet for a minute or so. In a few seconds he noticed it and started looking around for the source.

He looked up, he looked under the counter, he looked out the windows, he looked everywhere. A few minutes later, I did it again when he was bending down. Again he looked all over for the source. This went on three or four times and my partner and I were having trouble eating because we were trying so hard not to laugh out loud.

He walked away but soon returned with another busboy. He was telling him about the mysterious red light that appears and disappears. They both stood there for several minutes and the light did not appear, but the moment the second bus boy walked away, and the first bus boy bent down, naturally it reappeared. He called the second bus boy back and told him he had it figured out. It only appeared when he was bent down. Yes, you guessed it, both of them bent down looking for that red light.

At that point we paid the check and left.

Part of my duties as a detective involved bringing prisoners to bond court, and I'd usually end up going about twice a week. It's a pretty boring part of the job and sometimes you would have to sit for hours waiting for your case to be called. Naturally to pass the time a little, the laser came to court with me.

For a period of about three to four months I had one of the bond court-room deputy sheriffs completely stumped by that mysterious red light. In this case I would just aim the laser on the floor in front of the sheriff's office door and occasionally move it around a little. I would do it only when she was the only one who could see it.

She would come out of the office, look at the ceiling, check the alarm sensor, and look at the clock and light fixtures. As time passed, she would ask others in the courtroom if they saw that light. No one ever did.

The gag ended one day when she saw the red dot and called another deputy sheriff out to see it. I turned it off when the other sheriff came out of the office. She kept him there for several minutes, telling him that red light was back today and to watch the floor. When he had enough of looking for that red light and turned his back, I again turned it on right in front of her on the floor.

She shouted out, "It's back, there it is!" Everyone in the courtroom stopped and looked at her. She ran back in the office. I almost fell out of my chair.

My favorite laser story took place in Gulf Shores, Alabama, where we were staying in a condo that overlooked the Gulf of Mexico. It was just at dusk one evening and I was standing on the balcony, looking down at the beach. I was curious to see if my laser would work on the white sand from seven floors up. Did it ever!

There was a little girl, I would guess to be five or six years old, playing in the sand behind her parents. I aimed the light a few feet from her and it got her attention immediately. She chased it and tried to step on it several times, before she told her parents. When her parents looked back I turned it off. This went on for a few more minutes until we both ended the gag.

She snuck up on the elusive dot and caught it by covering it with her inverted sand bucket, at which time I turned the laser off. Then she ran off to report the capture to her parents. She brought them back to the bucket and lifted it very carefully only to reveal that the red dot had somehow escaped.

LET'S GET PHYSICAL

"What is comedy? Comedy is the art of making people laugh without making them puke."

--Steve Martin

Let's face it. The human body is a pretty amazing machine. So when normal things don't look quite right or don't sound quite right, it can lead to some pretty funny moments. Here are a few of those moments that have worked for me.

Booger Nose

Sometimes when I'm in a small group, I'll turn away from them to cover a (fake) sneeze. When I turn back, they're grossed out to see that I have a rather large greenish drop of mucous coming from one nostril.

I know this is really gross, but it is a real attention getter. The booger nose gag can be purchased in most any novelty shop. It is a light greenish-yellow plastic drop with a small flared bulb on the top to hold it in your nose. It runs (no pun intended) about a dollar, and it looks exactly what it's intended to look like. I buy them by the dozen (wholesale), as I tend to lose them. I think my dry cleaner has retrieved several over the years from my pants and jacket pockets. The odd thing is, he never asks about them.

From time to time, while giving a police seminar, I will do the fake sneeze bit, and then turn around with the booger hanging from my nose. Most of the time the officers will just start laughing, but sometimes they just stare at me with very bewildered looks, or look away from me.

Occasionally, an officer sitting up front will try and motion to me about the problem, pointing at his nose and gesturing to me.

For years I have wanted to put the booger in my nose on a really cold day and then make a traffic stop. One of these days before I retire, I think I will try it.

Ballpoint Nostril

I've been known to fiddle with a ballpoint pen and then, just when everyone's attention is appropriately focused, I create the illusion that I stick the pen up my nose.

I know, this is pretty gross too…but it always creates a really interesting reaction from those who view it.

I first got the idea for this gag from a Tenyo magic trick that had a gimmicked pen. The pen looked like a regular "Bic" type, but the cap had been cut in half, allowing the lower part of the cap to slide up and down the barrel of the pen, while the top half of the cap stayed in place on top of the pen.

To create the illusion, hold the pen by the lower part of the cap in your hand between your thumb, index and middle fingers, with the cap side down. Put the other end slightly into your nose against the side of your nostril. Gently push up on the lower part of the cap and slide it up the barrel of the pen, allowing the pen to slide down into your hand, hiding it. The illusion is perfect. At this point all that remains is to make an awful face, as the pen appears to be going up your nose.

I often do this while in casual conversation or while lecturing. I generally pick up the pen and start fiddling with it, scratching my face and nose, then I just stick it up my nose.

Be careful when doing this gag, don't actually push the pen into your nose. That would not be funny, and you'd be the first to know it.

Neck Cracker

While talking with friends, you mention you neck has been hurting, but that you have found you can relieve the pain by cracking your neck.

You then proceed to use your hands to adjust your head during which time a rather loud crackling sound occurs. It really sounds like every bone in your neck is going through some horrible realignment. It's another of those unexpected sounds that make people wince. I like it for that reason alone.

I first learned about this device many years ago at Billy Bishop's magic shop in Riverside, Illinois. It is really nothing more than a child's toy. I am not even sure what they are called. Basically, it's a piece of a hollow, ribbed, flexible plastic tube about four inches in length and one inch in diameter that can be compressed to about half that size. It's during the compression that you get the cracking sound. I found some of these toys in the form of a toy telescope at a surplus store. As I recall they were priced under a dollar.

To work the gag, start with the tube at its maximum length and have it hidden in your right hand. Put your right hand behind your neck and place your left hand on your chin. With your left hand, turn your head and with your right hand compress the tube. At the same time, put a painful expression on your face.

I have used this gag in almost all of my lectures, speeches and talks for the past five years. It always plays very well and gets a great reaction.

Next time you're in a toy store, it is worth seeking out one of these items. If you have small children, you might already have one of these lying around the house. If so, take it from the kids and use it properly.

Eye Popper

Imagine sitting around with friends at dinner or while giving a speech and being able to pop your eye out with a soup spoon and have your eye balance in the bowl of the spoon, while leaving a gaping black hole where your eye was.

The "Eye Popper" is a trick I purchased from a magic dealer, and I suspect most any magic dealer can get one for you. Because this is a magic trick and is commercially manufactured and sold, I won't reveal exactly how it works. I do encourage you to buy one if this type of material interests you.

This is an easy-to-operate gag and, as you might expect, always elicits gasps and groans from those watching this grossness. Naturally you really don't pop your eye out because that would limit your performances to just two, but the illusion created looks exactly like you did.

The most common response I get from this gag is, "You are really sick!" That, of course, is music to my ears.

Back Cracker Simplified

Here's another version of the back cracker gag. While talking with friends, you put your right hand behind your back and your left hand on your side. Then bend forward slightly, and as you start to stand up straight, a loud pop or crack comes from your back.

James Randi, magician, author and debunker of psychics and faith healers, first taught me this. It's a very simple, but effective, gag. All you do is snap your fingers on your right hand as you start to stand straight. This is an excellent impromptu effect.

Cracking Your Fingers

As you are standing or sitting around with friends, you grab your fingers one at a time and crack each one very loudly.

I saw a magician do this at a magic convention recently, and saw another magician do it years ago.

35

Hold your left hand palm up. Grab one of the fingers on your left hand and completely cover it with your palm down right hand, wrapping your fingers around the finger. Then push down slightly and, at the same time, snap your right index finger (or middle finger) and thumb. You can go right down the line, snapping all four fingers, one right after the other.

Watch your angles on this. It's important to keep the angle of vision such that those watching cannot see you snapping your fingers.

Women sometimes will gasp or give a little scream at this one. Most people will just look at you like you are very strange.

Don't overlook this one; it is great.

Flashing Red Ears

Can you imagine standing around, talking with friends, when all of sudden one or both of your ears light up red? If you've read this far, I guess you could.

This is another new item I just discovered. You can purchase it at any novelty or magic store for about $10. Tell your friendly dealer you want to buy some "Fire Ears."

The outfit consists of two small red lights, each attached to small clear plastic hook that hangs over the back of your ears. A thin wire runs from each bulb to a small battery and switch pack. The wire runs down the back of your shirt and then down one of your sleeves. The battery switch pack hangs from your sleeve into your hand.

The battery switch pack has two switches, one for each ear, so you can light them independently, together or have them alternate.

I have not played too much with this yet, but thought it would be funny to just have your ears blink red while talking with people. I also think they could be used as turn signals while walking. For my friends in law enforcement, they could be used while out of the car on traffic stops for added safety. I can hear you now: "Yeah, right."

Warm Regards

You are with friends at a bar. You excuse yourself to go to the restroom. Upon returning you grab one of your friends by his arm or hand and tell him, "Whew, I almost didn't make it in time."

At the same moment, your friend senses the warm, wet feeling on his arm or hand that just came from your hand. Yikes!

This was taught to me by a police officer a long time ago. Yes, I know this is really gross, but I assure you it can be quite funny. This is another one of those gags where it's vitally important to pick the right time, the right place and the right victim. Some people take this gag better than others. I'd hate to see you get punched out over a joke. When I choose to do this, I'm pretty confident about the reaction and the outcome. You should be too.

To set this up properly, make sure you tell the people you're with that you are going to the restroom. Before leaving the restroom, run some warm water on one of your hands, but don't dry it. Walk up to the person you are going to victimize and grab his arm, if he's wearing a short-sleeve shirt, or hand with your wet hand and say, "Whew, I almost didn't make it."

The look on their face is usually priceless.

JUST FOR COPS

"The aim of a joke is not to degrade the human being but to remind him that he is already degraded."

--George Orwell (1903 – 1950)

I know the chapter heading says, "Just for Cops," but of course it's not. It's just that all these gags and stories happened to fellow officers at the Franklin Park Police Department or to other officers attending one of my seminars. It seemed like a good way to collect these incidents. With minor modifications, many of these gags are adaptable to your particular work environment.

What's That Clicking Noise?

A co-worker is sitting at his or her desk and, when the office is quiet, starts to hear strange, erratic clicking noises. The noises will last for weeks or until your co-worker discovers the source, whichever comes first.

The source is Mexican Jumping Beans. A few times a year you can buy these at various stores. Purchase the ones that come in a plastic container. Make sure you check out the display in the store and pick up some active ones. Next tape the plastic container under the desk or in some other out-of-sight spot near their work area. I have found the best place to put them is taped to the bottom of a desktop, over the drawer.

I came up with this idea about 10 years ago. Here are my two favorite stories:

At the time, one of the detectives I worked with was Bob Andris. Bob fell for this one big-time. I had taped the container under his desk as described. At the time, I was working days and Bob was working evenings. The next day when I came to work, the chief's secretary came into the office and told me what happened after I left.

It seems Bob heard the beans clicking and could not locate the source. He called the chief's secretary in to try and help him. A few minutes later the village mechanic was walking by the office and he was summoned to help. It seems the three of them searched for a while and eventually gave up when the clicking stopped. This drove Bob crazy for several days until he finally found the plastic box.

Another time, I taped them under the chief's desk. (Yes, I admit that I sometimes have a lapse in judgment as I pursue these gags.) It was making him crazy for a day or so, until he happened to mention it to his secretary, who "spilled the beans" to him.

Not Loose Change

You walk up to a vending machine and see several coins lying on the floor. Naturally you go to pick them up, only to find them glued to the floor while several nearby people are laughing at you.

This is an old gag that goes back at least half a century. It was advertised as a Nail Nickel in the old novelty catalogs, but those coins had nails soldered to them that you actually nailed into the floor. This is better and causes less damage.

All you need is a couple of coins and some "Crazy Glue," (a wonderful invention). Be careful of what type of floor surface you do this on. "Crazy Glue" can damage some types of flooring. I have only done it on concrete and ceramic tile floors. I have done this many times over the years, but I have gotten into trouble a few times too.

The incident I recall most vividly is getting a call from the chief one day. He asked me to come to his office, "right now." There I was standing in front of the chief's desk and he asked, "Do you know anything about those coins being glued to the floor in front of the pop machine?"

I replied, "Maybe."

The chief said, "I thought so. I did not think it was too funny when I tried to pick them up at shift change with two shifts of officers standing around. You have five minutes to get them off the floor."

I beat his timetable by three minutes.

10,000 Envelopes

Several years ago I did this on the gag on the spur of the moment and it turned out to be a remarkable gag they still talk about at my department.

My boss at the time, Rocky Fortino, had ordered two boxes of 500 envelopes for our office. Somehow while it was going through the labyrinth of ordering, approvals and purchase orders, the order got screwed up. On the morning when the envelopes arrived, we got two boxes all right, two boxes of 5,000. We now had 10,000 envelopes. All day long, Rocky was upset since we had no place to store 10,000 envelopes, nor could we return them as they had been printed with our return address.

It was quitting time for me and as I getting ready to leave, the 3 p.m.-11 p.m. shift detectives came in. The idea hit me. I grabbed an envelope from my desk and handed it to Bob Andris who was just coming on duty and told him we were almost out of envelopes and said when Rocky is done with his meeting (he was in his office with the door closed at the moment) to tell him to order some more. When I came in the next morning, Rocky just looked at me and said, "We need to order more envelopes, huh?"

Later that day when Bob came in he sat down, looked and me and said, "Thanks, I needed that!"

Hideous Masterpiece

This is a gag that just evolved. I was at a surplus store one day and came across a bin of 18" blank wooden desk name plaques. They were triangular with each of the sides being about an inch in height. I had no idea what to do with them, but I bought a couple on speculation for fifty cents each. Then the idea came to me.

We had a new detective in the office and he needed a name plaque for his desk, so I thought I would help him out. He had a rather long last name, so I made up one of the plaques with his title and first and last names using some red stick-on vinyl letters. It looked awful, but it needed even more.

So I added a small American flag on a stick to each end of the plaque and then picked up (from the surplus store, again) a small gold-plated eagle that I think came from the top of a trophy. I screwed that into the center of the name plaque. Then I fastened two of our department's patches to sticks and positioned them between the flags and eagle. It was a masterpiece and looked absolutely hideous.

I knew if I put it out on his desk, he would toss it in the garbage right away. So I did the only other reasonable thing I could do. I would only put it out when he was not at work. This worked out great because we were working different shifts. When I was working days, I would put it on his desk as soon as I got in and put it away just before he came in. When I was working evenings, I would put it on his desk right after he left and put it away when I left.

The reaction of people coming into our office was hilarious. You couldn't avoid seeing this monstrosity. Some people would just stare at it, others would ask about it. I would always keep a straight face and just shrug my shoulders when asked about it.

This went on for over a month until the inevitable occurred. One of the officers in our department came in the office and asked him where that goofy-looking name plaque of his was.

"What name plaque?" he asked.

"You know – the one with your name, the gold eagle, the patches and flags."

Needless to say, he initiated a search of the office, found his name plaque (in my desk, of all places!) and the joke was over.

Should he ever forget about it, somewhere I still have a few photos of it sitting proudly on his desk.

Head Quarters?

I do this during a break from instruction for an audience of police officers.

I borrow two quarters and stick them to my forehead. Then I ask, "What is it?"

After I receive a variety of guesses and answers, all of them wrong, I give them the answer: "Police Headquarters."

After the moans and groans stop, I tell them, "Who are you kidding, half of you will do this as soon as you get back to your station." Most of the cops nod in agreement.

All you need are two quarters. You just put them on your forehead, side by side. The natural oil from your skin will hold them in place for a short time.

This is gag I came up with about 10 years ago. Obviously it only plays for cops, but I suppose if you are not a cop and your business has a head-quarters, you could adapt it. Don't overlook this. I know it sounds corny, but it is funny. And I've always heard that a groan is as good as a laugh.

Quarter On the Head

After you have shown the Police Headquarters, put one of the quarters back on your head and ask, "How does it stay there?" Again, after I receive a variety of responses (some quite unusual I might add), I remove the quarter and show it to have a large roofing nail attached to it.

You need to glue a roofing nail to the back of a quarter with "Crazy Glue." I find that roofing nails work best as they have a rather large head. To set this up, palm the quarter, with the nail, in your right hand as follows: Place

43

the quarter between the base of the index and middle finger. The nail portion will then lie across the base of the middle and ring fingers. Next, you pick up the real quarter with your right hand and stick it on your head. When you are ready to remove the quarter from your forehead, do so as follows:

Grab the real quarter from your forehead, on the bottom side, by pinching it between your right index finger and thumb. While doing this, nod your head down. Then, relax your grip on the quarter with the nail by slightly opening all your fingers and spreading your index and middle fingers, which will cause the nail with the quarter to fall out of your hand. At the same moment let the real quarter fall downward into your hand.

The illusion is that the quarter that was on your forehead just fell though your hand. I always have someone cup their hands under my hands so they can catch the quarter with the nail. If you allow it to hit a table or the floor, it can break the nail off the quarter.

I learned this about 30 years ago from a magician friend, Dale Delsandro. I have used it ever since and found it to be the perfect follow-up to "Police Headquarters."

I recall that on several occasions after I did this bit, people would take a long look at the quarter with the nail, then take a long look at my forehead and say, "You didn't really have that nail stuck in your head, did you?"

New Paper Punch

This is another one of these gags that just seemed to happen. In our office at the department we had just one, three-hole paper punch. It was quite old and was kept in the corner of the office on a desk.

Every morning my boss, Rocky, would have to leave his office, walk to the paper punch, punch some reports and return to his office. One day the punch was missing and Rocky said that's it, I am getting my own paper punch.

A few days later his new paper punch arrived and he no longer had to leave his office to punch holes in the reports every morning. The old paper punch was still missing and no one knew where it went.

The next day the old paper punch reappeared on the desk in the corner and I saw one of our tactical officers using it. I asked him where he found it.

He told me it was right here on the desk. Then I figured I would have some fun with him. I told him Rocky had bought us a new paper punch, but would not put it out until the old one was turned in to him.

This guy fell for it and took immediate action. He picked up the old paper punch, walked into Rocky's office, picked up the new paper punch from his desk, replaced it with the old one and started to walk out. Rocky was on the phone at the time and just watched in amazement.

As I recall, the guy just about made it to the door before Rocky had a few words for him. The next thing I heard was, "But Bruce told me............" Just then, I suddenly remembered that I had some interviews to conduct and got out of there.

Raining Paper

I discovered that those little paper holes from the paper punch could be really messy. Couldn't that lead to problems in the wrong hands?

One day I was emptying out the little paper dots from the paper punch in the office. I thought it was a waste to throw away all those paper dots when an idea came to me. One of the detectives kept his small, fold-up umbrella in the office.

With my partner's assistance, we opened the umbrella, dumped all the paper dots in and closed it. A month or so went by.

Then I came to work one rainy day and noticed little paper dots all over the ground right outside the back door of the police station. I would have paid to see the look on his face when he opened that umbrella. He never said a word about it, nor did I.

A few months later, the paper punch needed emptying so I filled his umbrella with those little dots again. Once again I came to work one rainy day and saw paper dots all over the ground by the back door.

He never said a word about it, but from that point on, he kept his umbrella with him.

Check In Here

Every Thursday in our building, traffic and misdemeanor court would be held at 9:30 a.m. and 1:30 p.m. When you walked through the front doors of the station, the courtroom was directly in front of you. As a matter of fact, there were several signs indicating that was the courtroom. It was hard to miss.

Nonetheless, it seemed that every Thursday, some people just did not see the signs or figure out that they were looking right at the courtroom. They would inevitably stop at the records desk and ask the clerk where the courtroom was. This irritated one particular records clerk to no end. She eventually made up a sign that said "Courtroom" with an arrow pointing to it, which she placed on the window to her office every Thursday.

One day she was complaining about all this to me which was probably a bad idea since, of course, that gave me a good idea. I went back to my office and made a sign reading, "Check in here for court." The following Thursday, when she was not looking, I put my sign over hers. I then sat in the hallway and watched.

At least half the people coming in tried to check in with her, showing her various papers and asking her all kinds of court-related questions. At one point she had a line of about 10 to 12 people waiting. She finally came out of her office and told the line of people to go to the courtroom and check in. Then she turned around and saw my sign. How can I say this? She was not pleased.

I don't know if she ever figured out for sure that I had made up that sign, but I know she suspected me.

I guess I was a highly rated candidate on a lot of suspect lists. Most of it was deserved.

Radioactive Waste

A few years ago I had stopped in a local surplus store and came across some large yellow plastic bags with the words "Radioactive Waste" imprinted on them. I bought several. The bags sat in my closet for a few months until I came up with an idea.

I put a few handfuls of peat moss in one of the bags and brought it to work. I found the building maintenance man and asked him to help me out. He agreed, but since his English was somewhat limited, I don't think he fully understood what the joke was about.

At any rate, I tore a small hole in the bottom of the bag and pulled some of the peat moss through the hole. I then asked him to carry the bag into the records room and show it to the records clerk, while telling her he had found this in the parking lot and did not know what it was or what was written on the bag.

He did exactly that. As I watched from the hallway, the records clerk first had a very puzzled look on her face, followed by a look of surprise. Unfortunately, I could not hear what she was saying, but I saw her pointing at the bag and then pointing outside.

At that point the maintenance man started laughing. The records clerk came out in the hallway and spotted me immediately. She told me later that somehow or another she knew I was involved and would not be far away. Maybe it's because I was glowing.

New Laptops for the Detectives

I was sitting in my office one day when one of the sergeants came in just to talk a bit. He noticed an empty box for a laptop computer lying in the office. We were going to use the box for bait on a case we were working on regarding some internal theft occurring in a local company.

The sergeant asked what the box was for and my partner and I told him all the detectives were getting new laptop computers to do our reports on. He was kind of surprised since we had all just received new typewriters the month before. He said that was nice, and asked what we were going to do with the typewriters. He said the patrol division could really use them.

I don't know where these thoughts come from, but we told him the village office clerks were going to get them. When he asked why, we told him in a gentle, roundabout way, that the village felt the patrol officers were too stupid to work these new high-tech typewriters. He had a fit and stormed out of the office.

49

We thought that was the end of the joke until about a week later when I was called into the lieutenant's office. It turns out that at a staff meeting earlier in the day this particular sergeant got up and said it was really nice that the detectives were all getting new laptop computers. He then mentioned that he thought it was unfair the village clerks were getting the detective's typewriters because they felt the patrol officers were too stupid to work them.

The chief asked him who told him all this nonsense. He replied, "Walstad and ....." and then immediately realized he had been had. I received a warning from the lieutenant to stop making up all these absurd stories. The following day the sergeant in question came in the office again and actually laughed about the whole incident.

Speak Up, Officer

You can only guess at how many gags were played during the years I was in the detective's office. You'd probably guess low.

One of my favorite things to do was mess with the other guy's phone. Taping the receiver button down, taping the handset down and leaving strange voice mail messages went on all the time.

My favorite gag was unscrewing the mouthpiece and putting pieces of black paper over the microphone. This muffled the voice. The more paper you added, the more muffled the voice became. Over a period of several months I would add one piece of paper a week to this one guy's phone. I would hear him talking with people and continually raise his voice as they were telling him they were having trouble hearing him.

This ended when the phone repairman came out to fix several miscellaneous problems with various phones around the station. The detective whose phone was not working well told the repairman about his problem, and the repairman discovered all the pieces of black paper in the mouthpiece.

For me, that was another trip to the lieutenant's office.

Bob's Bulletin Board

Bob Andris was a detective in our office and one of my former partners.

Bob had a bulletin board right behind his desk that he didn't use. When I would find odd phrases and headlines from magazines and newspapers, I'd always cut them out and pin them on Bob's bulletin board. They were things like: "Johnson Family Reunion," "Hanover House," "Norris Files," "No Win Situation" and so on. I had been doing this for months and basically Bob just ignored them.

One day I was sitting in the office talking with the chief when he started reading Bob's bulletin board. The chief looked at me and gestured to Bob's bulletin board and asked what was all that about.

Trying not to laugh, I told him I had no idea. Then the chief said, "What, is he cracking up?"

It was all I could do to keep a straight face.

Word Game

I am not quite sure how, when or why my partner Norm and I started this game. It was a challenge that we used to play on the phone when both of us were in the office.

Whenever one of us would be on the phone, the other guy would write down a word or short phrase and hand it to him. That person would then have to incorporate that particular word or short phrase into their existing phone conversation.

I recall a few words and phrases that we used included, "bushel baskets," "bowling," "mason jars," "candy," "badminton" and "wheelbarrow." The more unusual the word, the tougher it became to incorporate.

This got to be quite interesting and almost comical at times. I can still see Norm sitting at his desk working the word "badminton" into a conversation with another detective from another town. "So was his daughter active in any sports, like tennis or badminton?"

The game sharpens your mental and verbal agility. Norm got to be really good at the game. It's a fun bit of business; try it.

I must conclude by saying that we never played the game during a serious conversation, or while talking with complainants or witnesses.

Stop Office Pen Theft

If co-workers continually go into your desk and "borrow" one of your pens and then conveniently forget to return them, they might think twice about that habit if, occasionally, one of the borrowed pens exploded.

This is a standard item you can find at most novelty or magic shops. They cost a buck or two. The pen doesn't really explode, of course; it has a small mechanism that sets off a small cap when the cap of the pen is removed.

For years I was constantly missing pens from my desk drawer at work. It was usually another officer who needed a pen in a hurry and just grabbed one to write a note, and it then somehow wound up in his or her desk or pocket.

One day when I was in a magic store, I saw the demonstrator pull this gag on another customer. I immediately saw the possibilities, bought two on the spot, along with a good supply of caps.

Back at work and before leaving for the day, I would put all my real pens out of sight and place the exploding pen right in front. The next day I would come in and check the pen. It was amazing how often I would find the pen had "been used." From time to time someone would complain to me about that pen. A few times the pen simply disappeared; I suspect a surprised and annoyed pen "borrower" tossed it in the trash.

As time went on, the word went out: Stay out of Walstad's desk, he has it booby-trapped, things explode, alarms go off and so on. In time, I all but eliminated my missing pen problem.

I discovered that there is a potential downside to this gag. A few times I caught the wrong victim. On two occasions, the chief was sitting at my desk and went to use a pen. You guessed it: Bang!!!

I was glad that both of these incidents occurred on my days off.

If you are not up to using exploding pens, then just load your desk drawer with pens that are out of ink or broken.

"Pedro" Is Missing

One particular lieutenant, who worked at our department several years ago, had a habit of leaving his personal coffee cup all over the station. The cup

had a face sporting a large mustache on it. The lieutenant named the carica-
ture on his cup, "Pedro."

Several other officers and I kept seeing the cup in various places and
finally decided to have some fun with the lieutenant. Every time we found it,
we would take it and find some unusual way to return it to him.

One time we found Pedro far from home, so we placed it in the desk
drawer of another detective. We took a Polaroid photo of it in there and
placed the photo in an envelope with a ransom note. We had the envelope
delivered to the lieutenant at shift change. Just by looking at the photo, the
lieutenant knew the photo was taken in our office.

The detective (whose drawer we had put Pedro in) had just come on
duty and had just sat down at his desk when the lieutenant came in with the
photo in hand. He walked down the row of desks until he found a match. He
opened the drawer and there was Pedro.

The detective whose desk it was in pleaded innocent. The lieutenant
knew he had been set up, but gave him the business anyway.

Pedro was returned in several other memorable ways too. Once, the
lieutenant noticed the cup missing, only to have Pedro arrive a few days later
via UPS. Another time Pedro was "missing in action" and somehow got
wrapped in a couple of rolls of duct tape and left in front of the lieutenant's
door. The lieutenant was not happy that time.

Occasionally Pedro would be kidnapped and the kidnappers would send
ransom demands along with photos of Pedro. Pedro appeared in various
photos, showing him bandaged, or with a gun to his head, with tea bags in him
or next to a newspaper showing that he was still OK on that particular date.

Pedro even spoke once when the kidnappers had Pedro make a tape
with the ransom demands. This routine went on for a couple years, but as
time passed the lieutenant would become more careful about leaving Pedro
lying around.

In the end, it was the lieutenant himself who did Pedro in. He accidentally
dropped poor Pedro on the floor and the gag came to a shattering conclusion.

All in all, the lieutenant took the gag quite well and I think he actually
enjoyed the game. I know we did.

Walstad Standard Time

Whenever I would watch military and police movies I always noticed that in the background of some shots they had four (or more) clocks showing the time in various parts of the world. It gave me an idea.

At a local drug store one day, I found some battery-powered clocks on sale for $2 each, so I bought four. That night at the station I hung all four clocks on the wall in our office and put a label below each one: Paris, Tokyo, New York and Franklin Park. Then I set each of the clocks with the appropriate time.

It was funny to watch the expressions on people's faces when they came in our office and looked at those clocks. I wonder if they thought we really needed to know that information.

Box 2389

About 10 years ago, our police station was being remodeled. As far as I could determine, no one within the police department really seemed to know exactly what work was being done. A few officers and I got into that discussion several times. Wishing to prove my point one day, I got a piece of chalk and wrote on the wall in our old records room: "BOX 2389 HERE" and then drew a rectangle around it.

For the next two months I watched the wall as the remodeling continued all around it. No one put anything in front of it and, as far as I know, no one asked what Box 2389 was.

The finale came one day when some boxes of equipment were being delivered and moved into that room. When the delivery men stacked some boxes in front of the wall where the writing was, the chief – who just happened to be standing there at the time – told the delivery men to move their equipment, as a box was being installed there.

Moving Desk

For several years we shared our office with the training and crime prevention officer. He was a real picky guy and constantly complained to everybody about everything. I'll admit that we used to torment this guy at every opportunity with a variety of gags and jokes.

His work area was against a wall and he would sit with his back to the wall facing the office area, with his desk in front of him.

The funniest thing we ever did to him was simply to move his desk. It actually took him quite a while to realize we had moved his desk, since we only moved it about a quarter- to a half-inch at a time. About once every week or so, we would slide his desk back a little. The joke ended after about six months when he tried to spin his chair around and it hit the desk and the wall.

He got up, looked around and it was like seeing a light come on over his head. He ran to tell the lieutenant what we had done.

Then he moved his desk back to its original position, marked the position of the legs on the floor and measured the distance between the desk and the wall. About once a week we would catch him measuring things to make sure we had not moved it again.

Dropping Desk

I've had co-workers in my office accidentally bump their desk, only to see it shake, move and then drop about an inch and a half. It's fairly noisy and more than fairly amusing. You'll need to invest a dollar in this one, but believe me it's worth every penny. Literally.

I came up with this idea a few years ago, and I've set it up several times.

You need 100 pennies and a friend to help you. Make four equal stacks of twenty-five pennies. Place one stack next to each of the desk legs, each on the same side of the legs, e.g., each stack would be placed on the front side of each leg.

Next, carefully lift the desk and balance the legs on the stacks of pennies. It may take a few tries and restacking until you get it right. No one will notice that the desk is slightly elevated or moved over an inch.

Now when someone bumps into the desk or pushes away from it, it will move off the pennies, slide slightly, shake a bit and drop the inch and a half. This is guaranteed to get their attention.

Be careful when you're selecting a desk. Make sure it is sturdy and that this stunt won't damage the desk. Those standard metal desks that are common in all offices are the best. Also, select a desk that is not touching a wall or other furniture. You don't want it moving into a wall as it drops or into other piece of furniture, or pinching a co-worker.

I did this once to another detective at work. I was working evenings and he was working days. My partner and I set it up before we went home. When we came in the next day, the guy we did it to said nothing and acted like nothing had happened. Later we found out what really happened.

It seems he was sitting at his desk, talking with Lieutenant Fortino and a sergeant. He pushed away from his desk, which went shaking and sliding, then dropped the inch and half to the floor. He jumped up against the wall behind him with a look of horror on his face.

Fortino, who was talking at the moment, watched the whole incident, shook his head and kept right on talking. The sergeant started laughing and the detective began cursing my partner and me.

Visitor's Pass

When you visit some police departments, you are required to wear a visitor's pass. Our small department did not require them. But I thought we should, so I made one up.

It had our department name and logo on it, along with a number and the words "Visitor Pass" in boldface type. I had it laminated and attached it to a pin. My favorite target of this gag was the state's attorneys who would come to the department to approve charges and conduct interviews in the more serious cases.

When they would come into the office, I would tell them the chief is around and he wants all visitors to wear the pass. I can still picture a few of them walking around the station with that pass pinned on their shirt or blouse. I remember one day a female state's attorney who was working on a case with us was at the station. Naturally she was wearing the pass. A short time after her arrival, the chief came back to my desk and asked me what on earth the state's attorney wearing. (How and why he singled me out I will never know.)

At that moment she walked into our office. In spite of my usual ability to keep a straight face, I had to turn away to keep from laughing, as did the chief. She knew something was up so the chief went up to her and asked for the pass. He then handed it to me, and walked out shaking his head.

To this day, that state's attorney will remind me of that incident. I'll bet over the years, that pass was worn by at least 20 different state's attorneys.

Watchful Goose

Years ago, I purchased this very realistic, life size, goose puppet. There was a rod at the bottom of the goose that you used to make its head move from side to side. It was amazingly lifelike, especially when its head turned. I had planned to use it in my children's magic shows, but one evening it found its way into the office.

I brought it to work to show my partner and a few of the guys at the station. I was walking down the hall, operating the goose's head and making it look from side to side, when I passed one of the interview rooms. At the time, I didn't know that another officer had a DUI arrest going on in that interview room at the moment.

A few minutes later I walked back, with the goose looking around, passing the interview room again. A short time later I heard the DUI suspect loudly complaining about something or another to the arresting officer. Then I heard him say, "...and make that goose stop looking at me."

My partner and I almost fell out of our chairs laughing.

A Salt...

Here's a quickie that you can use when you're sitting at a restaurant table with a bunch of other law-enforcement types, waiting for your meal to arrive.

Pick up a saltshaker with one hand and a knife in the other and ask, "Does anyone know what this is?"

After everyone has given up, say, "It's assault (a salt) with a deadly weapon."

There's about a one-second delay before the moans and groans start.

(Yes, it's corny, but you'll use it and so will all your dining companions next time they're out for a meal.)

London Calling, Old Chap

Lt. Dennis Marlock, one of my friends and a fellow police officer (now retired), of the Milwaukee Police Department often complains about this one. I had pulled a series of gags on Dennis via the phone and mail and he was becoming a bit gun-shy of any unusual phone calls or letters. It's funny how this stuff can make one paranoid.

Anyway, one day Dennis received a phone call from Constable Barry Crichley from London, a bobby he had been corresponding with. The caller spoke in a flawless English accent. Well, Dennis thought I was up to another phone prank and immediately started making fun of the constable's accent and then made a few off-color remarks. To say the least, the caller seemed quite puzzled by Dennis's behavior and language.

After a few minutes, realization hit, and Dennis figured out it wasn't me and was indeed Constable Crichley calling from London. Dennis called me later that day and gave me an earful over a gag I never did.

Sometimes I'm innocent.

Letter from Kentucky

Detective Tom Rinaldo of the Buffalo Police Department, a friend of mine, is known to pull a good gag now and again himself. Tom also lectures on carnivals and carnival game fraud. Tom and I have presented a few seminars together. One day I decided to have a little fun with him.

Tom received a lengthy, rambling, disjointed letter from an 85-year-old retired deputy sheriff living in rural Kentucky. The letter explained that he used to inspect and close all the crooked carnival games that came into his county. He further explained that he had confiscated all kinds of crooked carnival games over the years and wanted to give them to Tom. The letter included a detailed list of all the games. (Just an aside here: Original crooked carnival games have become valuable collectors' items, so Tom was getting really excited about acquiring all these treasures.) As Tom continued reading, the deputy sheriff wrote that he would need a trailer or truck to haul all the games back to Buffalo.

In spite of all the detail about the carnival games, there was only one detail missing. It seems the last page of the letter with the deputy's address and phone number was missing. The letter was postmarked from a small town in Kentucky, but somehow the return address label had been scraped off the envelope during transit.

I let a week go by and then I phoned Tom's secretary. She had been the victim of many of Tom's gags and was more than willing to help me out from her end of this bit. I told her to leave Tom a note telling him this deputy sheriff had called for him. When Tom returned and found the note, he questioned his secretary why she had not taken down his return phone number.

She told Tom, "The old guy said you already have it."

About a week later I phoned Tom's secretary again and told her to leave another note that the guy had called back. She said she would.

A few days later Tom called me. He told me he had just gotten back from Kentucky with a whole load of carnival games. I couldn't take it and burst out laughing. So did Tom.

Then he told me about his numerous attempts to locate the retired deputy and how he finally got his secretary to confess and tell him about the gag.

Here are a few details on the set-up: When I prepared the envelope to Tom, I put one of my return address labels on it. Then I tore most of it off, leaving only one edge of it. I scuffed up the envelope with my shoe where the label was, making it appear that it had been torn off in transit. Then I put the postage on it, put it in another envelope and mailed it to a police officer I know in Kentucky, with a note asking him to re-mail the letter to Tom.

If you have a friend who's a collector (of anything), keep this scheme in mind. With just a few minor adjustments, it'll work for you too.

The Hoagland Files

Jim Hoagland was a great policeman, a master practical joker and a good friend of mine. Over the years Jim and I worked together in the patrol division we pulled our share of really great gags on other officers. There are too many to include here, and some were a bit too gross and/or risqué to write about. Those I've included below are among my favorites from our time together.

However, I must add here that we also did what I feel was some really good police work. Jim caught more burglars than any police officer I have ever known. He taught me a lot about police work, in addition to pulling a good gag. Jim Hoagland died in 1990. The world lost a really nice guy and a great police officer. I lost a good friend.

Flowers in Winter?

Imagine waking up on a cold winter morning to discover that all the flowers in your flower boxes had bloomed and that flowers had grown all over your yard.

This was one of Jim's brainstorms and it was certainly the most colorful gag we ever perpetrated.

One night about 1:00 a.m., I received a radio call from Jim to meet him behind a particular factory. When I arrived, I found Jim standing in a large dumpster filling up boxes with an incredible assortment of plastic flowers.

It seems this factory did something with plastic flowers and had thrown out thousands upon thousands of odd plastic flowers, stems and leaves. I helped him fill several boxes and then we enlisted the help of another officer. We all drove to the home of another officer on our shift who was off that day.

For the next hour we planted flowers everywhere in his yard – in the flower boxes, in the flowerbeds, along the sidewalks and along the driveway. We must have planted at least a thousand flowers that winter night.

At first light we all returned and observed our handiwork. We all agreed it was quite colorful.

The next day when the officer returned to work he had a few choice words for Jim and me. It seems his neighbors all found the display quite amusing. He also mentioned that his wife was not too happy about all the new gardening.

Set for a Luncheon

This is another gag that Jim and I pulled. Jim came across several boxes of paper tablecloths, paper napkins, paper plates, paper cups and plastic silverware. His first thought was to call me at the station and tell me he had an idea. I knew it was going to be good.

In the squad room at the department we had three long lunchroom type tables. Jim and I rearranged the tables into a "U" shape and proceeded to set the table with all the stuff Jim had scavenged. We added a few vases with some of the leftover plastic flowers and it looked perfect. No one else knew we had done it. For two days no one touched anything, thinking it was set up for a luncheon or something.

Eventually we heard the chief asking what all this was about. He did some checking, found out no one had anything planned and everything was thrown out.

Traffic Stop

Here is another one of Hoagland's gags. Jim and I made up a fake cardboard vanity license plate with another officer's nickname on it, which I will not mention here. We attached it over the rear plate on his car.

We figured he would notice it right away and we would all get a little laugh over it. Well, he did not notice it and went home, parked his car and went to bed. Later that morning, his wife went out shopping and – you guessed it – the police in another town stopped her for the phony license plate.

From what we heard the next night, the officer who stopped her was quite understanding and helped her remove the phony plate. It seems that once he found out her husband was a policeman, he fully understood.

Fine China - Handle With Care

Jim and I came up with an idea to have some fun with a new female officer in the department who had just moved into a third-floor, walk-up apartment.

Somewhere Jim had come across a discarded toilet bowl. We packed the toilet in a big carton that had shipping labels still on it. We simply changed the name of the sender to a china company and addressed the package to her. We added some labels that read: "Fine China - Handle With Care" and "Extremely Fragile." We were all working the midnight shift at the time and after work, Jim and I went to breakfast. We knew she would be asleep by this time, so we went to her apartment building and placed the package in the entrance foyer of the building.

That night she came into work and really gave us an earful. She explained that she had gotten up in the afternoon and was going out when she noticed the package. Somehow she carried the heavy package up the three flights of stairs. Then she carefully opened it and found the dirty old toilet bowl.

To make matters worse, it seems that her mother was with her at the time. Then she went on to tell us how she carried the toilet back down the three flights of stairs.

We were flushed with pride.

Caught Sleeping

Every so often, when working the 11:00 p.m. to 7:00 a.m. shift, an officer will park in an isolated area and close his eyes for a few minutes and sometimes doze off. It is just one of things that occur when you work midnights; you can never get enough sleep at home. I learned early on that the trick was not to get caught resting your eyes by the sergeant or, even worse, your fellow officers. If you were caught you were fair game for just about anything.

Jim Hoagland and I had a few gags we would pull if we spotted another officer dozing. Our favorite was to sneak up on him and place an empty five-gallon bucket against the front and rear bumpers of the squad. When the guy would start to drive off, in either direction, he would hit a bucket, stop and go the other way and hit the other one. It never damaged the car, but would never fail to get the officer's attention.

One of the best gags we ever pulled on a dozing officer was one fall night. Jim had come across a Halloween mask of an old man with long white

hair. We stuffed the mask with newspaper and inserted a coat hanger. We rigged it so the mask hung from the light bar by the coat hanger, right in front of the driver's-side window, with the face of the mask looking in the car.

We found the officer we were looking for dozing behind a factory. We snuck up on the car, hung the mask on his light bar and left.

That's one gag that I wish Jim and I had been around for to observe the final result. All I can tell you is that this particular officer did not talk to us for days after that.

DRINKING & DINING

"Humorists always sit at the children's table."

--Woody Allen

Because of the nature of police work and my seminars in other cities, I often find myself in coffee shops, restaurants and occasionally (after work and post-seminar) in lounges. I've found that these locations are wonderful for many of the gags in this book.

Fork It Over

While sitting with friends at dinner, you ask someone sitting across the table if you can sample something on their plate. When they say yes, your fork suddenly telescopes out to about two feet in length and you reach onto your friend's plate and grab a piece of food.

This is an item you can find at most novelty and magic stores. It's called a telescopic fork. You can also find a version using a soup spoon. They cost a couple bucks each.

I have used these for some time. Some people see the humor in this gag, but others do not appreciate you reaching onto their plate of food.

For that reason, I have stopped actually taking their food. Instead I just deliver the line, expand the fork and then just rest the tines of the fork near their plate. It gets a good laugh and no one is offended.

Pad of Dollar Bills

You're out with friends at restaurant or coffee shop. At the cashier's counter to pay your check, you pull out your checkbook, but inside is not checks, but a pad of dollar bills. You tear off the appropriate number and pay the cashier.

This is another great gag that has been around for awhile. I could not tell you where I first learned this, but I think I read it in a book somewhere a long time ago.

Here is how you make this one up. Go to your bank and get a number of brand new one-dollar bills. I usually get 50. Next, put them on a dollar-bill sized piece of light cardboard, put the package in a vice and brush the top (long) edges with rubber cement. Let it dry and you'll have a finished product that's basically a note pad made of one-dollar bills. Put them in a checkbook and they're ready to use.

I get mixed reactions from this. Some people will just take the bills, look at you quizzically and put the bills in the cash drawer. Others are more suspicious and will hold the bills up to the light or mark them with the counterfeiting detecting pen and look at you strangely.

Many will ask, "What's this about?" or "Where did you get these?"

I reply, "This is a new thing the Treasury Department is doing. They make these up in pads of ones, fives, tens, twenties and combination pads. You can get them at any bank."

I always imagine these people going to their banks and asking for a combo pad of money.

Cracking Your Teeth

Quite often when I'm sitting around a table at a restaurant or in someone's home, I stop whatever story I'm telling to take a drink of water. Just as the glass reaches my mouth (and usually all eyes are on me at this point because I just paused in my story), there's a loud "crack" that sounds as if the glass broke, my tooth broke or both. People invariably wince and say "ouch."

It will work with a bottle just as well as a glass.

Jay Marshall taught me this one at least 25 years ago. It is one of my favorite dinnertime gags. All you need is a large coin, at least a quarter but preferably a half dollar or a silver dollar. I prefer the dollar as you can get a louder noise. Here's how it works.

Secretly get the coin from your pocket and place it in your right hand, holding it on the fingers. Then pick up the glass with the same hand, with your fingers at the front of the glass and your thumb at the back, just as you would normally hold it.

Now without anyone seeing you, position the coin between the front of the glass and your fingers and very slightly clip the upper edge of the dollar on your index finger. At this point, your hand is holding the coin against the glass, with the fleshy part of your index finger keeping the coin from making full contact with the glass. The upper edge of the coin is slightly exposed at this point but don't worry, no one will see it.

Now, as you start bringing the glass to your mouth, push on the coin with your middle and ring fingers. When the glass just about reaches your lips, move your index finger up. This will release the coin, which will click loudly against the glass.

Then use your acting ability to jerk your head back, yell out, "Aahhh," and with your left hand quickly cover your mouth.

The standard reaction from those who just observed this is, "Are you OK?" or "Ouch, I'll bet that hurt!" or they will just shake their heads and give you a look.

I was showing this to a room full of cops one time and as I was finished explaining the gag, one of the officers added to the idea by suggesting that after you crack your teeth and yell, you spit out several white "Tic Tac" breath

mints. You can easily put them in your mouth when you bring your left hand up to cover your mouth. I have since used that ending.

You will need to practice this a few times to get the timing down. Also, be careful not to really hit your teeth with the glass or bottle, I know it really hurts, and there is a possibility of doing some dental damage.

Lucky Napkin

Free drinks happen more often when you've got a little "edge." It might be right under your drink.

While you're sitting in a bar or restaurant with friends, you turn over your cocktail napkin and find it to be imprinted with the following message:

Lucky Napkin
Redeem for One Free Drink

Is this your lucky day or what? You motion the waitress, waiter or bartender over and show them your good fortune.

Go to your local stationary shop or printer and order a rubber stamp with the above-mentioned phrase. The one I use is a self-inking stamp with red ink. The imprint size is 2" wide by 1" high.

This is really a new one for me. Earl Reum told me about this at a magic convention we were attending in Colorado in September 2000. He gave credit to another magician who he saw use this some years ago. As soon as I returned home I was off to the printer to have one made.

I have used this only a few times, but it has had very positive results. When in a restaurant (or bar) with friends and the drink order arrives and the server leaves, I pick up a few of the drink napkins and stamp them and turn them upside down and replace the drinks on them.

The reaction from those sitting with you is almost as funny as what is going to happen next. When the server returns, you or someone else at the table brings attention to the stamped napkin(s).

The reaction ranges from, "I don't think so," to, "Where did you get this?" to "I wish they would tell me about these promotions before they start them." Most everyone has figured out it was a joke and they laughed along with us. By the way, I have never accepted the free drink when the server thought it was for real.

Another way to use this is to take three or four of the imprinted napkins and "salt" the stack of napkins on the bar by putting them in at every 20th position or so. When they turn up later that night or even the next day, you won't be around. The problem with this is that you'll miss seeing all the fun.

You could also put just one in the stack, maybe two or three napkins down from the top and imprint side up, and let the bartender discover it as he's putting out napkins for the drinks.

Let me offer a word of warning here. You are on your own with one. Use discretion. If the bartender wants to give you a free drink because you're a good customer, a fun guy or because he enjoyed the gag, fine. Accept it with thanks, and don't forget a nice tip when you leave. I would advise not pushing the issue of a free drink. I suspect one could be asked to leave the establishment if you became too demanding.

Cash From Coasters

While you are at a restaurant or bar with friends, you casually tear open the drink coaster to reveal a folded one-dollar bill. When they ask about it, you explain that it's a new promotion that the bottler (whatever company name is imprinted on the coaster) is doing.

Then sit back and watch how fast your friends will start tearing up coasters. In many cases so will the staff of the establishment.

I have been doing this gag for at least 25 years. The working is simple. All you need is a new or fairly crisp newer bill. Fold it in eighths and hide it in your palm. Next, pick up the coaster and place it over the bill in your palm. Now tear the coaster open from the center and slide the bill under the tear. Then reach through the hole and pull out the folded bill.

In thinking back on all the times I have done this, it is probably one of the gags that gets the best reaction from onlookers. For example, when I was in Connecticut conducting a seminar, I went to dinner one evening with Lt. Jim Salzano. After we ate, we retired to the bar area for a cigarette and a drink.

I did this gag in front of Salzano and the barmaid.

Salzano, who had seen me doing some of my zany material during the day, caught on at once, but the barmaid went for it hook, line and coaster. It worked out perfectly because the barmaid explained to us that the beer company that gave them the coasters actually ran some sort of promotion a few months ago where the coasters had a punch out middle and you could get free drinks. We couldn't have asked for better timing.

The next thing we knew, the barmaid and waitress were in the garbage pulling out all the coasters and tearing them open. The manager came by and asked what on earth were they doing.

They told him about the "new" promotion and just think of all the money they had been throwing out. We left shortly thereafter.

FILE UNDER 'MISCELLANEOUS'

"In the end, everything is a gag."

--Charlie Chaplin (1889-1977)

There are always a few gags and bits of business that don't fit one of the other categories. That's why I created this Miscellaneous file. I think you'll find some good material in this chapter as well.

Christmas Cards from New Friends

It's a day in mid-December and the mail arrives. Wow, lots of Christmas cards to open. As you are opening them, you run across one of those photo cards with a picture of some children you don't know. You read the name and signature, and it's no one you know. You ask your spouse and children, no one knows these people, but they know you...or do they?

I'm not sure when I got this idea, but I have been doing this on and off for years. In admitting this, any of my friends who read this now know the source of those cards they got from strangers.

Every Christmas we all get those photo cards with pictures of families or just the children and sometimes just children with the family pet. After Christmas, I save them until the following December. Then I go out and purchase the proper size envelopes and address them friends who don't know my other friends whose photos appear on the cards.

I never have heard any reaction from anyone on this, but I suspect I will when this is published. I bet these cards had a few people wondering.

Mystery Postcards

Over the years, friends of mine have received postcards from various states from people they don't know. I could not tell you where I learned this, but I have used it for years just to have fun with people.

While on vacation, pick up cards from some of your various stops. Address them to your friends who don't know you are on vacation and sign them with a fictitious name. Mail them from the various cities you visit. It will make them really wonder.

Another variation is to have your friends in other cities buy some post cards for you and send them to you in an envelope. Now write a nice note on the post cards and again sign a fictitious name. Put the proper postage on the cards and return them in an envelope to your friend, with a note asking him to mail the postcards for you. This works great because your victims who know you will know you're not on vacation.

Out of Candy

Here is a Halloween gag I have used for years. When the trick-or-treaters would show up at my door, I would tell them I was out of candy and then offer them a variety of bizarre items instead. My favorites were things like dryer lint, a can of cat food, a rubber fish or a piece of string. I would generally only do this to older children about eight to ten years old as they reacted the best. The looks on their faces are priceless.

Some would look over their choices and actually select one of the items. Of course, then I would tell them I was only kidding and give them candy.

Trick or Treat

Here is another of my favorite Halloween gags. When the trick-or-treaters would come to the door and say, "Trick or Treat," I would ask them what did they want. See a trick or get a treat? Amazingly enough, almost all the kids asked to see a trick, which I would then proceed to do.

I'd do a quick magic trick for them, followed by some treats.

The only down side to this gag is, they keep coming back to your house wanting to see the trick again.

Lint and Thread Pickers

While you are standing around, talking with friends, one of them happens to notice a small piece of thread hanging on your shirt or coat. Most people invariably want to pick these things off and clean you up. As they pick it up and attempt to remove it, the thread keeps getting longer and longer and longer, and they never do find the end. They almost seem embarrassed because now it seems they're unraveling your coat!

This is another really old gag, and I cannot even recall the first time I heard of this.

To set this up you need a spool of thread, in a contrasting color to your shirt or jacket. (I find this works best with a suit coat or a sports coat.) Simply thread a needle with the thread and push it through your shirt or coat from the inside, near the shoulder. Remove the needle and you are left with a piece of thread just hanging on your shirt or coat. Place the spool of thread under your shirt, around the belt line or in one of the inside pockets of your coat and you're all set.

Walk up to friends or strangers and join in the conversation. Generally it only takes a matter of seconds before someone notices that

thread hanging there. I have found some people will look, but not touch. Others will see it and call it to your attention, but many others can't resist and will grab for it instantly.

As they start pulling on the thread, the spool unwinds and the thread gets longer and longer. It's quite funny to see how much they will pull before they realize they have been had.

Many years ago I worked with a guy who was a "close talker" and one of those people who had to touch you while he talked. He was also a lint, hair and thread picker. On several occasions I observed him talking to co-workers while picking at the lint, hair and threads on their shirts. He did it to me a few times and then I remembered this gag.

One day I came in wearing a dark shirt with the gag set up with a piece of white thread. I walked by him and he spotted the thread at once. He immediately started a conversation while he stared at that thread. It took him about 10 seconds and he went for it. He started pulling it and as it got longer and longer his look turned to complete amazement.

He actually got about three or four feet out when it dawned on him what was going on. He didn't say a word and just walked off fuming. Later he came over to me telling me how funny he thought the gag was and could I tell him how I set it all up.

I showed him the set-up and we remained friends, but after that he never picked at anything on my clothing.

When Was Edison Here?

Imagine going through your file of business cards one day and finding business cards belonging to Thomas Edison, Wilbur Wright, Henry Ford, Howard Hughes or some other noted individual. Believe it or not this happened to several co-workers of mine.

Several years ago, I saw a framed display of business cards of famous and noted individuals, like those just mentioned. One spot was empty and reserved for your business card. I got an idea. I bought the display and copied some of the business cards. I had a stack of each made up. Whenever we got a new detective in the office, I would add some of these cards to their new business card file.

If I knew I was going to another police department to see a detective I knew, I would always bring some of the cards along and, without his knowledge, add a few to his card case. Sometimes it would take months to find them all.

Wouldn't you think that if you pulled a business card out your file that read "Dr. Albert Einstein" that you'd remember meeting him?

This is an easy one to make up with you PC and a graphics program that can create business cards. Just use your imagination and have fun.

Here's a Note

You hand a friend or a co-worker a small card, saying, "I was supposed to give you this note." When they turn the card over it is indeed a note, a picture of a musical note.

I could not tell you where I learned this old gag. Over the years I have seen several variations of it. If you're in a group situation, like a banquet or a meeting, where you're meeting people for the first time, after they're introduced, you say, "Oh, you're (name). I've got a note for you." Then hand him the card. If the attendees are wearing name badges, it's a simple matter to look at the name, then walk up and say, "Hi, (name), I've got a note for you."

Leave one of the cards on the chair of a co-worker or your boss. Next time you see them say, "I left a note on your chair."

You can make these up on your computer with just about any graphics program that has a format for business cards. Just load a graphic of a musical note onto the business card template and print out a few sheets of business card stock.

I use so many of these cards (and always give them away) that I have them printed by the thousand at a commercial printer.

I have been using this gag for several years and it always gets a groan, sometimes a laugh. Interestingly enough, even people who groan at this one will ask to keep the card.

See What Little Johnny Saw

You introduce this gag by talking about an old carnival pitch item, simply a small card that when held to a strong light, "allows you to see what little Johnny saw on his sister's wedding night, when he peeked through the keyhole of her bedroom door." When anyone looks, they see nothing. Then you deliver the punch line: "That is exactly what little Johnny saw – nothing – as his sister had the light out."

Bob Brown, a good friend, magician and ex-carnival worker told me about this one. Bob described it to me and I made up some on my computer, again using a graphics program (Broderbund's Print Shop) using the business card template. The card I made up looks like this:

SEE WHAT LITTLE
JOHNNIE SAW
THROUGH THE
KEYHOLE OF HIS
SISTER'S BEDROOM
DOOR, ON HER
WEDDING NIGHT

HOLD UP TO A BRIGHT
LIGHT AND SQUINT
SLIGHTLY

Here again, I go through so many of these that I have them commercially printed by the thousand. Sometimes I will just leave a stack of the cards lying on a table and watch the people walking by.

Some of them will pick a card up, read it and then put the card right back down again. Others will pick one up and try to see "what little Johnny saw." Still others will pick one up, read it and then put it in their pocket, presumably to view it in a more private area. It's a great way to study human nature.

At a magic convention in Colon, Michigan in August 2000, I laid out a stack of the cards just outside the main door. A group of people all came out at once and at one point I had eight, count 'em, eight, people all holding up a card, looking toward the light and squinting.

At the time I was sitting on a bench with my friend Todd Robbins who called out to the group, "They work better if you face the East." Like a well-rehearsed precision drill team, all eight people swiveled ninety degrees to face the East.

We just about fell off the bench.

"10" Cards

Even if you're just an occasional airline traveler, you know how boring the mandatory safety demonstration from the flight attendants can be. I have no doubt that the flight attendants get just as bored delivering the speech. How about this for a change of pace?

At the conclusion of the demonstration, you and several people around you all hold up a paper, printed with a large number "10." It's just like scoring an Olympic event. The flight attendants all laugh as do most of the passengers in the general vicinity who can see what you've done.

This gag is the brainchild of Earl Reum of Denver. After Earl gets seated on the plane, he gets as many people as possible in his row or nearby to help participate in this gag by handing out the preprinted 8 1/2" x 11" size "10" signs he always carries with him. It's important, of course, for everyone to keep the signs hidden until the final "judging." Over the years, Earl has received countless bottles of complimentary wine from appreciative flight attendants for doing this stunt.

Earl does not limit this gag just to airlines. Usually, anytime Earl is a member of an audience, those around him are prepared ahead of time with "10" signs to hold up at the conclusion of a speech, lecture or presentation.

I really liked the idea of the "10" cards, but did not like the size. So again, I brought it down to business card size and printed up a stack on my computer. I have used this myself only a few times on an airplane, but have had some good laughs with it. Sadly, I have received no wine yet. Now that I think about it, since I shrunk the size of the card, I'll probably end up with one of those miniature bottles of wine.

I also use these cards if people start telling a really long-winded story. I will hand people sitting around me a "10" card and whisper to them to hold it up to the storyteller when he completes his story.

My First Radio Appearance

About 10 years ago, I made my first appearance on a Chicago radio show, Extension 720, hosted by Milt Rosenberg. The interview was going to be about con games, frauds and swindles. I was also going to plug *Sting Shift*, the book Lindsay Smith and I had just co-authored. Since Lindsay lives in Denver and couldn't hear the interview, he asked me to tape the show for him. I agreed.

The interview went OK I thought, but I was a bit nervous in the beginning. I had phoned Lindsay and told him I had taped the show and would be sending him a copy, telling him I was a bit nervous at the beginning. I was about to mail Lindsay his copy when I got an idea.

Why not make up a phony tape and have some fun with him? Lindsay had never heard the show and wouldn't recognize Rosenberg's voice. So the next night a guy from work helped me produce our own version of the Extension 720 show.

We had a lot of fun making the tape and then I sent it off. It arrived in his mail at a particularly busy time and he didn't have a chance to listen to it right away. On Saturday, though, he called me and told me he had to take his family across town for some reason, and he figured that would be the perfect time to listen to the tape. It was about a 45-minute drive, which was about the length of the interview. Perfect. I told him again how nervous I thought I was at the beginning of the program.

As they got into the car, his teenage kids, of course, were all clamoring to hear music on their favorite radio station, but Lindsay told them they were going to listen to an interview with Bruce instead. There was some minor grumbling but then they agreed. Lindsay started the tape and adjusted the sound level so everyone could hear.

"Milt Rosenberg" gave me a flattering introduction and you could hear some nervous coughing in the background. As I was starting to talk, I accidentally fell off a chair with a crash. I apologized and a few seconds later burped rather loudly, quickly explaining that I had a gyros sandwich for dinner. I then said the "f-" word. Lindsay couldn't believe what he just heard. He was trying to drive and may have swerved into another lane at this point.

Then I said, "Oops, sorry Milt, you're not supposed to say f--- on the radio, are you?"

Lindsay had no idea where this was going next so the "interview" ended abruptly right there as he pulled the tape out of the cassette deck. Then, while his kids were listening to their music, Lindsay reconstructed what I had done and enjoyed the joke. He called me that evening, told me how all this happened while he was driving and we had a good laugh over it.

I really didn't expect to catch Lindsay's wife and kids in this joke but, as they say, things happen.

Page Two Letter

If you have a friend or relative that you haven't heard from for awhile, there's a guaranteed way to have them not only respond, but most likely they'll pick up the phone and call. It's called a "page two" letter.

Lindsay Smith first told me about this one, based on a page two letter he had received from the late Walt Rollins, a magician and friend of his in West Virginia.

The idea is simplicity itself. You apparently have written a letter to a friend, but he receives only page two. Here's an example of how the letter would start at the top of the page:

-2-

exactly what you've been looking for to add to your collection, and at an incredibly low price. But I wouldn't wait too long!

Sincerely,

...or try this one:

-2-

sending out dozens of resumes, including a few to several companies in (name of recipient's town).

Sincerely,

You get the idea. At the top of "page two," just start your sentence in the middle with some kind of arresting, eye-catching phrase that will make the recipient want to call you. Then put it in an envelope and mail it.

Your recipient's first reaction will be to look in the envelope again, thinking he somehow missed seeing page one. Then he'll think that you were in a hurry and simply forgot to include page one when you mailed it.

They'll call. They always do.

Dog Growls at Package

My wife went to some sort of store display and prop sale and saw three hunting trophies for sale for $5 each. Being the great wife she is, she bought them for me, knowing that I could figure out some kind of use for them. All three were ram's heads, were quite old and had a unique odor about them. Actually they smelled like goats. I was not quite sure what to do with them.

After awhile I came up with an idea.

I phoned my friend Dennis Marlock of the Milwaukee Police Department and told him I was sending him some recovered evidence from a con game that had gone down in our town. He asked what it was and I told him it was from a variation of the old Pigeon Drop scam. I boxed one of the ram's heads and shipped it to him via UPS.

A few days later he called and inquired what was with the ram's head. I told him that instead of using "found" money, these con men were using ram's

84

heads. He laughed and asked if I wanted my ram's head returned. I told him no, it was his.

He then went on to explain that his wife called him at work and told him that he had received a package from Bruce, and the dog was growling at it. When he got home from work, and after carefully opening the package and discovering the ram's head he put it in his garage. Until he pawned it off on someone else, his dog continued to bark at it every time he saw it.

Boy or Girl?

Those new gold dollars with Sacajawea and her baby on the face of the coin are really nice. They're not in widespread circulation yet, because collectors keep hoarding them. For that reason, people are interested in looking at them. This is a plus for you.

Show someone two of the new gold dollars, and ask if they know anything about them. Then explain that you heard the coins minted in Denver have female babies in the papoose and the ones minted in Philadelphia have male babies in the papooses. Then ask them if they can see the difference. When they move in nice and close for a look at the dollar you told them was the boy, it squirts them in the face (with a small stream of water).

The squirting coin gag has been around for years in the form of a nickel. It was only a matter of time before squirting gold dollars were available from the magic stores.

They sell for about $10. The instructions that come with the coin explain how to fill the coin with water.

To set this up, you need one squirting gold dollar, one real gold dollar and a small plastic case that both coins can fit in. You are now set to go along the lines described above.

In the first month of having this coin, I would estimate that I squirted at least 50 people, mostly policemen and firemen. What is really funny is when you are trying to set one person up for the gag and another comes along and sticks his head in the way so he can see what you are talking about. Needless to say, the intruder gets squirted.

You'll have fun with this.

CONCLUSION

OK…there you have it. Seventy-six of the best jokes, gags and bits of business that I've enjoyed using over the past several decades. Compiling the material for this book has allowed me to relive some genuinely funny moments of my life. I smiled, and even laughed as I recounted them. Many of these were just as funny to me the second time around. I hope you enjoyed them the first time. (Unless of course you recognized yourself in some of these; then it'll be the second time around for you too.)

Now then. In spite of my up-front disclaimer admonishing you not to do any of these things, I know that some of you will try one or more of these stunts. That's the reality. But here's some advice, and I think it's important:

Pulling a good practical joke relies on several factors. The most important are these: Don't damage anything or physically hurt anyone. If either of these occurs, it is not funny and you could get in trouble or beat up.

• If the description reads, read the instructions carefully, please take a few minutes to actually read the instructions. Believe me, it helps to know what you're doing.

• If the description reads, practice this before you do it, please practice. You'll feel more comfortable when you're working the gag and your results will be much better.

• If the description reads, pick your time, place and the victim carefully, please do so. Believe it or not, not everyone finds this stuff as amusing as you and I do.

• If the description reads, be careful using this, then please be careful. Accidents can happen. The whole idea is to have fun, not to cause problems.

If you come up with a really good joke or gag, please do me a favor and share it with me the next time we meet. I am always looking for new ideas and material.

I would like to thank all my friends who willingly or unwillingly contributed to this book. In particular I would like to thank Lindsay Smith. Besides being my best friend and someone who thinks all this stuff is really funny, he tirelessly edited this book and makes me look like I know how to write.

RESOURCES

Throughout this book there are numerous references to picking up various novelties, tricks or props – from cockroaches to fire wallets – at your local magic store. I encourage you to do this. Magic stores will soon be among your favorite places to visit to see "what's new." If you're in a city of any size, check the Yellow Pages listings under "Magic Shops" or "Magician's Supplies." The dealers will be eager to help you locate exactly what you're looking for or show you something else that's equally amusing. Tell them Bruce Walstad sent you. If they say, "Who?" ask them if they're carrying this book. If they're not, have them call the publisher. (Make sure they call before you complete your transaction.)

In the book, I mention several stores by name in reference to specific items. Here is additional detail on those stores.

Al's Magic Shop (Al Cohen)
1012 Vermont Avenue NW
Washington, D.C. 20005
1-800-alsmagic

Dallas and Company (Andy Dallas)
101 E. University
Champaign, Illinois 61820
217-351-5974

Bob Little Guaranteed Magic
27 Bright Road
Hatboro, PA 19040
215-672-3344

Magic, Inc. (Jay Marshall)
5082 N. Lincoln Avenue
Chicago, IL 60625
773-334-2855

If you've decided that you really like this kind of nonsense and would like to take it to another level, I have several suggestions for you. OK, never mind that...here are some books and a videotape I can highly recommend.

Penn Jillette and Teller, *Penn & Teller's How to Play in Traffic*
Penn Jillette and Teller, *Penn & Teller's Cruel Tricks for Dear Friends*
Penn Jillette and Teller, *Penn & Teller's How to Play With Your Food*

If you thought some of the material in this book was tasteless, I must warn you that you haven't seen anything until you've read Penn & Teller's books. But then, you've seen Penn & Teller on TV or, perhaps, in person. So you know (sort of) what to expect. They're wonderfully inspirational and highly recommended.

If you liked the gags with a squeaker in this book, then you must obtain a copy of Doc Wayne's book on squeakers, *The Art Of Public Squeaking*. This is the definitive book on the subject. It even comes with the squeaker you'll need. In addition, Dan Garrett wrote a booklet on squeakers, titled *Squeakeasy*. This booklet contains over 50 ideas for using the squeaker. It makes you wonder, doesn't it? Two books written, just on the squeaker.

If you enjoyed the stuff you can do with the Funken Ring or Spark Ring, you need to pick up a copy of *Sparks, The Funkenring Book* by Brad Reeder and Bill Robinson. It is loaded with tips, gags and effects you can do with the Funken Ring.

The neck-cracking device described on page 33 also has a booklet devoted just to it: *Breaking Bones for Fun & Profit* by Tom Burgoon. It contains several ideas for handling and using the neck cracker. This booklet also comes with the neck cracker you need.

My friend Jay Marshall is the Dean of American Magicians, and a truly funny man with an encyclopedic knowledge of magic: history, antiquarian books, performers, vaudeville, puppets and marionettes, theatre, jokes and stories. Some years ago, Jay "starred" in a videotape appropriately titled, "Table Crap." As the title implies, this is a collection of jokes and stunts you can use to amuse your table companions when dining out or when you're invited to someone's home. It's hilarious material, and you'll be highly entertained even if you never use any of this stuff. If your local magic store doesn't have a copy, order it direct from Magic, Inc. in Chicago.

And thanks again for buying this book.

Index of Gags

F

H

I

L

M

N

O

P

Q

R

S

T

V

ABOUT THE AUTHOR

Bruce Walstad was born at a very early age in Franklin Park, Illinois. He came into the world clutching a Watch Winder. Shortly thereafter, his parents found a Whoopee Cushion hidden under the mattress in his crib. Ever since then, he has been expanding his repertoire of gags and practical jokes.

After a 25-year career in law enforcement – 15 years as an investigator – with the Franklin Park Police Department, Bruce retired in April 2001 to devote full-time to his already well-established seminar business.

Bruce is a recognized expert and one of the nation's leading authorities on confidence crime, frauds and swindles. Over the years, he has presented hundreds of training seminars to law-enforcement officers throughout the country on con games, carnivals and carnival game fraud, public speaking techniques, Gypsy and Traveler crime investigation, crimes against the elderly, and missing and abducted children.

Additionally, Bruce has also presented numerous talks and seminars for various businesses, groups, clubs and senior citizen organizations on fraud and con games.

He has appeared on many local and national TV shows including: *48 Hours, Oprah, Justice Files, You Asked For It, FOX News, Maury Povich, NBC News, Geraldo Rivera, Court TV, Discovery Channel, The Learning Channel* and *CBS News.*

Bruce has acted as a consultant on fraud and con games to most all network news and talk shows, and has testified in court proceedings as an expert witness on fraud. He is the co-author of two books for law enforcement: *Sting Shift, The Street-Smart Cop's Handbook of Cons and Swindles* and *Keeping Carnies Honest,* and has authored several articles on confidence crime for various publications, including *The FBI Law Enforcement Bulletin.*

He is a past president of Professionals Against Confidence Crime (PACC), an international organization of professional law-enforcement personnel who share information on confidence crimes and the con artists who perpetrate them, and continues to serve on its board of directors.

Bruce has had a life-long interest in magic, and is a member of the International Brotherhood of Magicians and the Society of American Magicians. He is an accomplished magician who has performed shows for children and adults throughout

The author at work.

98

the Chicagoland area. He frequently incorporates magic in his seminars to illustrate a point or just to entertain class members.

He lives in Franklin Park with his wife, Patti, sons John and Omar, and a kaleidoscopic assortment of dogs, cats and birds. Kramer, the Walstad's African Gray parrot, is something of a practical joker himself. Among other things, he does a wonderful imitation of a dispatcher on a police radio, including squawks and static. Now where would he pick up that kind of stuff?

About Street-Smart Communications, LLC

Street-Smart Communications, LLC, is a specialized publisher of information about frauds, swindles and confidence crime and now, it appears, practical jokes as well, for law enforcement officers, business managers and security personnel, magicians, collectors and others interested in scams and deceits for education or entertainment.

WHAT OTHERS ARE SAYING

What People Are Saying About *CAUTION PRACTICAL JOKER AHEAD*.

"This book is a hoot! The unique experience of actually holding an inspiration to action is magnificent. This book empowers people to entertain other people with a buoyant, excited sense of delight, which needs to be at least one element inside everyone's world. Funny is as funny does.

–Earl Reum, motivational speaker, Denver

"Great book! It is the best book I have ever read and written. I highly recommend it to everyone. In fact, you should buy two copies, in case you lose one."

–Bruce Walstad (author)

"I have known Bruce for more than 20 years. He is a great detective and a true master of mischief. I would have liked to have him work for me, but I suspect he would have gotten me into a great deal of trouble."

**–John Millner, Chief of Police
Elmhurst, Ill. Police Department**

"My husband has far too much time on his hands and this book proves it."

–Patricia Walstad (wife)

"I'm sure that none of the police stories in this book are true. I can't believe these things happened when Bruce worked for me. Anyway, that's my story and I'm sticking to it."

**–Rocky Fortino, retired Lieutenant,
Franklin Park Police Department**

"The sales of this book are helping to pay my college tuition. Please buy a copy for each of your friends. Oh yeah, the book is very funny."

–John Walstad (son)

"The author of this book, my dad, has taught me many things about life. Much of what he taught me is in this book."

–Omar Walstad (son)

"Bruce can nail you with a practical joke no matter where you live. Time and distance are not obstacles for him. He will reach across the miles and get you. Believe me, no one is safe…anywhere."

–Lindsay Smith, Denver